Social E
in Irelan

A People's Economy?

Edited by
Gerard Doyle & Tanya Lalor

OAK TREE PRESS

Published by Oak Tree Press, 19 Rutland Street, Cork, Ireland
www.oaktreepress.com

A catalogue record of this book is available from the British Library.

ISBN 978 1 78119 070 8 (Paperback)
ISBN 978 1 78119 071 5 (ePub)
ISBN 978 1 78119 072 2 (Kindle)

Printed in Ireland by SPRINT-print Limited

Contents

Contributor and editor biographies

Kieron Brennan is CEO of the Irish League of Credit Unions. Prior to joining the League, Kieron was Programme Manager with POBAL (which manages programmes on behalf of the Irish Government and the EU), Manager Ireland of Triodos Bank (one of Europe's largest ethical banks), Executive Director of Clann Credo, Chief Executive of Partas (which supports the development of local enterprise and the social economy) and Programme Evaluator with the European Social Fund Programme Evaluation Unit.

Bridget Carroll is a lecturer in the Department of Food Business & Development and a researcher in the Centre for Co-operative Studies at University College Cork. Her qualifications include a BA (University of Limerick), an MSc in Co-operative Organisation and a Postgraduate Certificate in Teaching & Learning in Higher Education (UCC). Currently, she is reading for a doctorate in co-operatives. Her research to date has focused on organisational, legislative and regulatory aspects of co-operatives. Bridget contributes to a wide range of undergraduate and postgraduate programmes, as well as outreach work.

Senan Cooke, PhD, has been chairman and founder of Waterford LEDC and secretary of DFBA Community Enterprises Ltd and Dunhill Rural Enterprises Ltd (County Waterford). He is also a founding member of Communities Creating Jobs, a national voluntary social enterprise dedicated to creating an open and collaborative environment in which its members agree to share ideas, solutions and best practices on how best to promote and develop both social and private enterprises in communities.

Anne Costello has been actively involved in community work since qualifying with an HDip in Community & Youth Work from NUI Maynooth in 2001. Anne was the co-ordinator for Clondalkin Travellers Development Group, a resource worker with the Community Platform (a network of 28 national organisations working collectively to address poverty and inequality) and has worked as a community worker with the Galway Traveller Movement, focusing on a number of issues including accommodation, education and enterprise. Anne worked in the private business sector in both Ireland and the UK before qualifying as a community worker. Anne has recently completed an MA in Applied Social Studies at NUI Maynooth, focusing specifically on the interrelationship between community development and social economy enterprises. She also has lectured for the Limerick Institute of Technology on its BA (Social and Community Studies) course.

Tom Daly is managing director and founder of TSA Consultancy, Ireland's specialist social enterprise development agency. Prior to that, he was the manager of the Social Economy Unit, a support structure for social enterprises in Tallaght, Dublin. Tom's special area of interest is cross-sector collaboration between public, private and community sector organisations for community benefit.

Gerard Doyle has 16 years' experience of working in community development and social enterprise development. He has worked for an area-based partnership company, a community development network in five communities in Waterford City, and Waterford LEDC, Ireland's first not-for-profit company involving the community and corporate sector. He works with TSA, where he has assisted a number of communities to develop social enterprise strategies. He has worked also as a part-time lecturer in community development in Waterford Institute of Technology. He holds an MSc in Local Economic Development from the University of Glasgow. His dissertation was on the impact that social enterprise could play in the regeneration of urban disadvantaged communities (available from www.tsa.ie).

Tor Justad has over 30 years' experience within the social economy sector, mainly in Scotland but also in several EU countries, including Ireland, Sweden, Finland and England. He has wide experience within the co-operative sector and has held a number of key posts within the sector, including Chief Executive of a regional community enterprise development agency. He currently works as a freelance social economy adviser.

Helen Kavanagh is the project coordinator for the ACTION pilot project, part-funded by the European Regional Development Fund through the Ireland Wales Programme 2007-2013 (INTERREG 4A). In managing the project, Helen engaged with many of the leading thinkers and practitioners in Ireland and UK while working on the ground with social enterprise promoters and employees in Ireland.

Erdmuthe Klaer-Morselli is Deputy Secretary General at the European Network of Cities and Regions for the Social Economy (REVES aisbl). Since 2005, she has been co-ordinating partnership-based activities of social economy and public authorities in different cities and regions all over Europe. She also is in charge of following related (legislative) initiatives of the various EU institutions and bodies. Before and after joining REVES, Erdmuthe has been active for many years in the associative and solidarity-economy sectors (fair trade) in Germany and Belgium. She studied communication and political science in Münster (Germany) and holds a Master's degree in European Interdisciplinary Studies from the College of Europe/Warsaw campus.

Tanya Lalor is a consultant in TSA Consultancy, and director of Irish Housing Associates (IHA Consultancy). She previously worked as a social economy advisor in the Social Economy Unit, Ireland's first dedicated social enterprise support unit. She also has worked as a researcher in the Graduate School of Business, University College Dublin, and also has lectured in the Dublin Institute of Technology and the Institute of Technology Tallaght. She holds a BA (Psychology), an MBS in HRM and Industrial Relations, and a Diploma in Social Integration and Enterprise for community development workers. She also has experience working in the youth and disability sectors in Ireland and the UK.

Olive McCarthy, BComm, MSc, PhD, is a lecturer with the Department of Food Business & Development and a researcher with the Centre for Co-operative Studies, University College Cork. Research interests include organisation and management issues, stakeholder participation in co-operatives, and performance measurement. Her research has been conducted mainly into credit unions, community co-operatives and agricultural co-operatives, on which she has published widely. She is the academic co-ordinator on the Diploma in Credit Union Studies and the MBS in Co-operative and Social Enterprise in UCC.

Margaret Ó Riada is a graduate of University College Cork, where she completed a degree course in the Applied Social Sciences in Community and Youth Work Practice. She believes passionately in the need for collective action to challenge inequality and proactively works to achieve this through her work as Co-ordinator of the Galway Traveller Movement. She holds a Master's degree in Law (LLM) in Economic, Social and Cultural Rights from the Centre for Human Rights, NUI Galway.

Deiric Ó Broin, PhD, is Director of NorDubCo, North Dublin's regional think-tank, in Dublin City University. Prior to coming to DCU, he was employed as an economic policy analyst in the private sector. He previously worked in the Office of Labour Affairs in the Department of Enterprise, Trade and Employment, and in the Office of the Tánaiste as a public policy adviser. His teaching and research interests include social innovation, public participation and public policy, and civil society.

Mary O'Shaughnessy, PhD, is a lecturer in the Department of Food Business & Development and a researcher with the Centre for Co-operative Studies, University College Cork. The topic of her PhD was survival strategies of rural-based social enterprises. She is a board member of the EMES European University-based research network on social enterprises and the HOPE Foundation; she also is a member of the National Rural Network and academic director of the NUI BSc (Hons) Rural Development by Distance Learning. Her research interests include rural development, social and co-operative enterprises.

Michael Punch, PhD, works as a lecturer in the School of Sociology in University College Dublin. Over the years, he also has been closely involved with community action in disadvantaged communities in Dublin, both through action research and voluntary consultancy. He is actively engaged with Tenants First, a cross-city network of local authority tenants' associations and anti-poverty groups working on housing and regeneration issues.

Martin Ward is a young Traveller man who currently manages First Class Insulation. He also runs a very successful catering business with his family. His personal experience of overcoming discrimination and racism in business is an invaluable resource to the Galway Traveller Movement, as is his innate ability to identify potential business opportunities suited to the Traveller community. Martin is currently undertaking a BA in Business, Enterprise and Community Development.

Chris White is Chief Executive of Boardmatch Ireland, Ireland's corporate governance charity. Previously, he was the Chief Executive of the Sue Ryder Foundation (the largest voluntary housing association in Ireland delivering housing to the elderly), and the Head of Development with the Irish Council for Social Housing.

Introduction

The concept of social enterprise has gained attention in recent years and increasingly is seen as one viable response to the economic trauma Ireland has experienced. This book aims to examine the concept of social enterprise, and what part it can play in the renewal of our economy and in addressing key issues facing Irish society.

SOCIAL ENTERPRISE AND THE ORIGIN OF THE TERM

The origins of the notion of social enterprise are associated with Italy in the late 1980s, when new co-operative initiatives emerged to respond to unmet needs, especially in relation to unemployment and the delivery of personal services (Defourny and Nyssens, 2008). One of the defining characteristics of these new co-operatives was their relationship to 'communities of interest' or specific geographic communities, compared with traditional co-operatives that were oriented primarily toward members' interests. Although the concept began to be used across Europe in the mid-1990s (Defourny and Nyssens, 2008), it has not gained the same recognition in all European countries.

As to what a social enterprise is, there is no universally accepted single definition (GHK, 2006) and the number of descriptions of social enterprise reflects a diverse understanding. The UK's Department of Trade and Industry's (2002) definition is widely used:

> A social enterprise is a business with primarily social objectives whose surpluses are principally reinvested for that purpose in the business or in the community, rather than being driven by the need to maximise profit for shareholders and owners.

The strength of the DTI definition is that it states that social enterprises have social and economic objectives. The principle of community ownership is alluded to but it does not place significant weight on the fact that social enterprises are managed differently than private enterprises in that they are democratically governed by a group of people on behalf of a community, rather than by shareholders seeking a return on their investment.

In an attempt to provide a comprehensive description of social enterprise, the European research network, EMES, formulated three economic and five social criteria (Nyssens, 2006).

The economic criteria are:

- **Continuous activity in the form of production and/or sale of goods and services:** unlike traditional not-for-profit organisations, social enterprises do not normally undertake advocacy work; instead, they produce goods and services.

- **A high level of autonomy:** social enterprises are created voluntarily by groups of citizens and are governed by them. Public authorities or private companies have no direct or indirect control over them, even though grant funding may be provided by these organisations.
- **A significant economic risk:** the financial viability of social enterprises depends on the efforts of their members, who have the responsibility of ensuring financial resources are either secured or generated from trading activity, unlike the majority of public institutions.

The social criteria are:

- **An explicit aim of community benefit**: one of the principal aims of social enterprises is to serve the community or a specific group of people.
- **Citizen initiative**: social enterprises are the result of collective interaction involving people belonging to a community or to a group that shares a certain need or aim.
- **Decision-making not based on capital ownership**: this generally means the principle of 'one member, one vote', or at least a voting power not based on capital shares. Although capital owners in social enterprises can play an important role, there are other stakeholders who influence decision-making.
- **Participatory character, involving those affected by the activity**: the users of social enterprises' services are represented on and participate in their structures. In many cases, one of the objectives is to strengthen democracy at local level through economic activity.
- **Limited distribution of profit**: social enterprises include organisations that totally prohibit profit distribution as well as organisations such as co-operatives, which may distribute their profit only to a limited degree, thus avoiding profit-maximising behaviour.

In identifying the trading aspect of social enterprise, EMES distinguishes social enterprises from traditional non-governmental organisations that are engaged either in advocacy or charity. Another distinction from many charities with donor-recipient relationships is that social enterprises should endeavour to promote the involvement of the users of the social enterprise on all levels of the social enterprise decision-making.

Social enterprises also are independent of the State, being formed and governed by a group of individuals associated with a specific community[1] and often on behalf of their community. However, their governance structures may include external expertise involving the State or the private sector, whose motivation is the development of the social enterprise.

SOCIAL ENTERPRISE AND SOCIAL ECONOMY

Social enterprises are part of the wider social economy, which can be defined as that part of the economy located between the private and public sectors, and which functions through independent organisations. The social economy is believed by the European Commission to account for approximately 6% of total employment across the EU.[2] At EU level, the social economy is seen to be made up of a family of organisations, sometimes referred to as CAMaF (an acronym of Co-operatives, Associations, Mutualities and Foundations). Ireland has a strong tradition of social economy organisations which, using the CAMaF framework, includes the GAA, the credit union movement, co-operatives, voluntary organisations, and community groups. The current status of co-operatives, their challenges and potential is discussed in **Chapter 12**.

IDEOLOGY

Different ideological approaches underpin and motivate the development of social enterprises. For some, social enterprise is an extension of the private and public sectors, and serves to fill a gap – often in services – that the private sector and the public sector do not meet. Typically, this can arise where the private sector cannot extract value (for example, market failure), and where the public sector either has withdrawn (for example, arising from policy or macro-economic forces) or does not recognise a need. This perspective has been characterised as the reformist approach.

For others, social enterprise is an alternative to capitalism and demonstrates a different way of engaging in economic activity. It is based on maximising the contribution of community and fostering their participation in decision-making. This perspective has been characterised as the radical

---

1 A geographic community, or a specific community of interest (those with a shared identity – for example, ethnic minority groups, marginalised groups, etc).

2 The Commission estimated 11 million EU citizens are employed in the wider social economy (http://europa.eu/rapid/pressReleasesAction.do?reference=MEMO/11/ 735, accessed July 2012).

approach (Pearce, 2003). **Chapter 2** describes how the emerging concept of social entrepreneurship is another ideological approach asserting that the many social problems in society can be addressed effectively by the interventions of individuals with private business sector skills and expertise.

The ideological perspective of individuals and organisations relating to social enterprise will influence the boundaries of activities in which social enterprises are likely to engage.

THE STATUS OF SOCIAL ENTERPRISE IN IRELAND

In Ireland, social enterprises are present in most communities, and include such services as community childcare projects, rural transport services, renewable/energy efficient projects, recycling enterprises and community cafés.

Little data exists in Ireland about the size of the sector: research undertaken in 2009 conservatively estimated that social enterprises in disadvantaged areas generated €240 million in revenue per year, employed over 9,300 people directly, and supported a further 5,100 indirectly (Clarke and Eustace, 2009).

However, there are difficulties in estimating the size of the sector: social enterprise is a relatively hidden concept in Ireland, and not all organisations involved identify themselves as such. There is little networking or association within the sector. This presents a difficulty for the sector itself: if there is a lack of engagement within the sector, a cohesive approach to its development is unlikely to develop.

As to why the social enterprise sector has not developed in Ireland to the same extent in other countries, there are political, economic and social reasons – some of these are outlined in **Chapter 1**. One of the factors influencing the sector is Government policy. Social enterprises have developed in spite of, rather than because of, State support. Currently, the State provides very limited financial support in the development of social enterprises. This contrasts with mainstream enterprise – according to the Social Enterprise Task Force,[3] support for private sector enterprise includes a budget of over €2 billion and over 28 tax breaks (SETF, 2010). Most of these enterprise supports are not available to social enterprises and there is no clear

3 Chaired by Maurice Healy (board member of Social Entrepreneurs Ireland and former president of IBEC), the Social Enterprise Task Force's membership includes social enterprises, support organisations, community practitioners, State support organisations, academics and experts.

policy framework for the development of the sector. The resources that are available for social enterprises have been primarily in the form of labour market programmes,[4] which undermine the development of a sustainable sector, as this policy perspective does not enable a vibrant and sustainable trading base to develop.

Such a policy perspective also has a constraining influence on how supports will be offered. **Chapter 4** describes the supports required for social enterprises and proposes how these might be delivered. The approach to supporting social enterprise and the influence that it can have on the development of the sector is discussed in relation to Scotland and Sweden in **Chapter 10**.

OPPORTUNITIES

In spite of the sector's limited development, there are many activities taking place in a range of sectors and there is significant potential: **Chapter 3** outlines the opportunities in relation to renewable energy and the green economy, and discusses the experience of Scotland and Denmark, where communities have had a significant role in the sector.

Chapter 6 describes how voluntary housing associations may be well placed to develop, as well as support, social enterprises and regeneration in communities.

In **Chapter 5**, the Galway Traveller Movement demonstrates how the concept can provide tangible benefits to communities experiencing disadvantage, such as the Traveller community in Ireland.

There are also opportunities arising from relationships with the private sector, through for example, corporate social responsibility (CSR) programmes. **Chapter 9** describes the relationships between communities in Waterford city and county and Waterford Crystal Ltd.

CURRENT AND EMERGING POLICY

There is an impetus at European level around social enterprise. In its Communication, the *Social Business Initiative,* the European Commission (2011a) stated that it "wants to contribute to the creation of a favourable environment for the development of social business in Europe, and of the social economy at large". *Social Business Initiative* also acknowledges the need

---

4 For example, schemes including Community Employment, and the Community Services Programme are regularly accessed by social enterprises to subsidise labour costs.

for a more inclusive form of economic growth, and states that social enterprises will be at the heart of this drive.

In December 2011, the Commission announced a proposed new investment priority in the ESF Regulation: the promotion of the social economy and social enterprises. Further financial support also will be provided over the period 2014 to 2020 through the Programme for Social Change and Innovation. Under this programme, nearly €100 million will be allocated specifically to promoting social experimentation, and another €90 million to supporting social enterprises.[5]

Chapter 11 traces the development of thinking within the EU around social enterprise, and considers what future measures may emerge.

At national level, the *Programme for Government* states that "The Government will promote the development of a vibrant and effective social enterprise sector" and adds "we will instruct agencies to view social enterprises as important stakeholders in rejuvenating local economies" (Government of Ireland, 2011), thus acknowledging the role of social enterprise in regenerating local economies.

It is argued in **Chapter 6** that the voluntary housing sector in Ireland is not only part of the social enterprise but can play a significant role in enabling social enterprises through procurement and support. The questionable success of public private partnerships, particularly in a regeneration context, as well as government policy on the primary role of voluntary organisations for the delivery of housing, further strengthens the case.

The Government's *Action Plan for Jobs 2012*, published in February 2012, gives a commitment to commission a report on the potential of social enterprise to create jobs:

> The report will identify the actions required, in funding, procurement, etc, by Government and other relevant bodies and agencies to create jobs in this sector. It will examine potential initiatives in this area (e.g. a Micro-Working Initiative) and will be prepared with particular reference to the European Commission's *Social Business Initiative* and associated funding. (DJEI, 2012: 67)

The role that procurement can play in supporting social outcomes and social enterprise will be crucial in the current economic climate, and it is argued in **Chapter 7** that greater value for money can be gained by the State in taking social considerations into account in the procurement process. This may be a

---

5 Commissioner László Andor, at the European Parliament's Social Economy Intergroup seminar on 'The social economy in the European agenda', Brussels, 8 December 2011.

critical means of support for the sector in the context of limited financial resources.

The economic context of Ireland provides an opportunity for communities to reconsider their relationship to their local economies, and to take an active role in shaping them, through social enterprise development, and there are many opportunities for this to occur. However, it is a mistake to think that social enterprises will flourish without specific supports being provided, including soft supports as discussed in **Chapter 4**. In **Chapter 8**, some of the barriers to social enterprises accessing finance are considered.

We hope that some of the key themes and issues discussed in this book not only will contribute to the debate on social enterprise, but will act as a resource to communities, policy-makers and those with an interest in the sector.

1 Social enterprise in context in Ireland

Michael Punch

INTRODUCTION

Ireland has a noteworthy history in collective economic development, as evidenced by well-known examples such as the co-operative and credit union movements. And yet, social enterprise remains relatively under-developed and limited in its political and cultural influence and its economic contribution to society. The situation is even more puzzling, given that the related notion of the social economy as an autonomous developmental sphere of importance has insinuated recent policy discourses at EU, national and local level to a considerable degree. There remain many open questions as to the real meaning, importance and potential of third-sector economic interventions in a global economy and within different cultural and institutional contexts. This is true conceptually (different actors have very different ideas and visions of what the social economy should be) and politically (a social economy for whom, by whom and to what ends?).

This chapter aims to contribute to the debate at a number of levels. It first builds a conceptual map of the diverse arena of third sector, alternative economic development. It then explores briefly the recent history of political engagement with development experiments in this field in Ireland. It concludes with some critical reflections on the meaning and possibilities of social enterprise, particularly in the context of the recent boom-bust cycle.

MAPPING ALTERNATIVE ECONOMIC SPACES

We need to start with a question of language: it is important to differentiate economic life according to its diversity of actors, imperatives, processes and relations (Gibson-Graham, 2005). Conceptual clarity on this point is crucial as there are many diverse alternative economic spaces.

One space of activity involves the local development of alternative economic models built around the consumption needs of households or communities. This includes the household economy, one of the "unstructured aspects of productive life", which revolves around the informal work of domestic life (Pahl *et al.*, 1983: 121). Informal economic activity also may extend beyond the household, as voluntary networks of support and care are constructed around kinships, friendships or communities of interest (Mingione, 1991; Friedmann, 1992). This wider world of work often is wrongly ignored in cultural assumptions and policies regarding labour markets and employment (Social Justice Ireland, 2012).

Autonomous spheres of development also may involve broader and more formalised collective efforts to explore and implement innovative practices and institutional arrangements in pursuit of alternative visions and values (egalitarian, ecologically sound, transformative, etc.), that put people and life to the forefront (Leyshon *et al.*, 2003). The terms 'social economy' and 'social enterprise' have been adopted in many quarters to denote a core area of activity of this kind. In general terms, the social economy derives from community or co-operative efforts to create alternative local development initiatives, which operate on a non-profit basis, incorporating a broad aim of independent control over economic activities directed towards meeting the material and socio-cultural needs of everyday life (Moulaert and Ailenei, 2005).

These dominant and alternative spheres of economic activity can be summarised diagramatically (**Figure 1**).

Figure 1: Mapping Dominant / Alternative Space Economies

Economic spaces:	Market ◄ Commodified		Non-market ► De-commodified
Economic sector:	Private	Third Sector/ Social Economy	Public
Core imperatives:	Accumulation, expansion	Autonomous development, mutual aid, empowerment	Redistribution, Social reproduction, Social control
Institutions:	Capitalist firm/enterprise	Social enterprise, community organisation, household, etc.	State institution

There is a constant interplay between State and non-State institutions, and in particular, the State is always engaged in the productive activities and reproductive requirements of the market (for example, legal regulation, bank bailouts, etc), though the nature, purpose and consequences of this engagement will vary geographically and historically (O'Neill, 1997). For example, the State typically pursues non-market interventions and the provision of social/de-commodified goods and services.[6] At the same time, there is a strong tendency towards commodification in the market, whereby goods and services are given both a use-value (qualitative worth) and an exchange value (quantitative worth – that is, how much goods or services can fetch in market exchanges). By this process of commodification, market relations become increasingly central to the processes of production and

6 One of the effects of neoliberal and third-way ideologies has been the further blurring of these qualitative differences between State and private actors in the economy; this has seen States adopting increasingly market-oriented approaches and discourses within a 'business model' of governance.

consumption, societies take on an increasingly consumerist orientation and greater parts of everyday life are drawn into the global process of capital accumulation – making money out of money (Harvey, 2000). This dialectical intertwining between capitalist economy and culture – between accumulation and ways of seeing and being – is expressed in the deepening penetration of everyday life by materialism, consumerism and individualism.

This field is further complicated by the third space of informality, which exists on a continuum between private capital and State enterprise. This alternative economic space can be distinguished through its characteristic imperatives (such as mutual support, empowerment), relations (reciprocal or co-operative), institutional forms (households, community organisations, social enterprises, etc.), activities (care-giving, community and social services, neighbourhood improvement, housing provision, advice and advocacy, etc.) and geographies. Each also may encapsulate essentially different values – for example, building a needs-based or people-centred development as opposed to one focused on economic growth and capital accumulation within distant institutions.

It should be remembered that these dominant and alternative economic spaces exist relationally within a continuum (or within a complex and dynamic 'whole' economy) – for example, community organisations may offer goods or services on the market or enter into contracts with private firms. Moreover, much third sector activity depends to some degree on State support. Nevertheless, the idea holds that, albeit unevenly developed and subject to advances and setbacks, there are social, economic and cultural possibilities outside of the dominant or formal processes of capital and the State. Critically, the precise balance between these diverse areas of economic activity will vary historically and geographically in line with changing structural and cultural factors.

THE SOCIAL ECONOMY AND IRISH DEVELOPMENT

In the Irish case, the key structural and cultural factors that have shaped the third sector economy over recent decades include wider patterns of uneven economic development, dominant political ideologies, State policy-making, and the balance between individualism and communitarianism. Ireland's social and physical landscape has been radically reconfigured since 1958, when the State began to pursue a programme of modernisation, introducing a development model based on export-oriented industrialisation, supply-side policies (for example, grants and infrastructural investment, no restrictions on profit repatriation, low tax on capital) and inward investment by foreign capital (Drudy, 1995; O'Hearn, 2001; Kirby, 2002). The consequences of this strategy included a deepening penetration by, and considerable dependence on, transnational capital and the realignment of the place of the Irish economy on a world stage, as the country increasingly took on a number of niche roles in global commodity chains such as pharmaceutics, electronics and a range of producer services. As is well known, the decade or so up to 2007 saw record rates of economic expansion, while the subsequent downturn (reflected in negative economic growth trends, rising unemployment, the crisis of financial institutions, and the property slump) has been sharp and painful. This boom-bust cycle was underpinned by neo-liberal macroeconomic and fiscal policies, financial deregulation, social partnership models of economic policy formulation, mobile transnational capital, and property speculation.[7] At the level of culture and ideology, the tides of consumerism, materialism and individualism, and the pressures these placed on traditional ties of community and solidarity, also were important explanatory factors in the Celtic Tiger saga. These cultural trends were deeply intertwined with the political economy of neo-liberalism.

The space and nature of third sector development also has changed considerably, and the social economy, in particular, has been given a small but noteworthy role (at least on paper) as a policy response to some of the inequalities of recent decades. Of course, it should be remembered that bottom-up economic activity has a long history in Ireland. In one way or another, and to varying extents, people always have turned to informal, household, and community economic strategies to survive and to achieve some measure of empowerment in the flux and stress of economic change. For example, the co-operative and credit union movements have a long history and national prominence, amounting to a substantial area of third sector economic life. The former, driven by visionary enthusiasts like Sir Horace Plunkett, George Russell and Tom Finlay SJ, had considerable success from the late 19th century in introducing co-operative models of production within dairy farming (initially) and then other branches of agri-business. This

7 The property sector, particularly housing, went through more than a decade of price inflation driven by demographic change, rising incomes and especially lucrative speculative activity, partly fuelled by government policies including tax incentives for property development. This sector constituted a considerable part of the boom economy with construction accounting for 13% of total employment in 2007, while housing investment alone accounted for 16% of gross national income. Much of this apparent economic contribution may have been fictitious, however, in that various estimates suggest that Irish house prices have been overvalued by anything from 30% (IMF, 2008) to over 100% (Drudy and Punch, 2005).

was an interesting success, given that the prevailing culture often was thought to be individualistic and therefore likely to be fallow ground for such co-operative economies (Bolger, 1977; Kennelly, 2011). The origins of the credit union movement lay in a similar period with the establishment of agricultural credit societies, though its notable period of expansion came in the 1950s (with the beginnings of a system of low-cost credit for urban and rural workers and communities) and 1960s (particularly with the *Credit Union Act, 1966*) (Quinn, 1999). However, the absence of any significant socialist or syndicalist political tradition at local and central levels arguably has meant that co-operative or social enterprise models have not significantly influenced mainstream development policies.[8]

Nevertheless, over recent decades, the nature of autonomous development of this kind has become more diverse and fine-grained with the evolution of a complex social economy and local development infrastructure. In particular, there has emerged a political faith in bottom-up, area-based (and, therefore, partial rather than universal) anti-poverty and regeneration strategies at EU and national levels. This has translated into a stronger local dimension to some European and Irish economic development policies and labour-market initiatives, the rationale for which derives from the need to address the spatial outcomes of economic restructuring and to identify new sources of jobs, particularly in the provision of informal services (Walsh, 1998). Examples include the EEC Poverty Programmes (1974-1990), the Community Development Programme, Area-Based Partnerships, Community Training Workshops, the Community Employment (CE) Scheme, Whole-Time Jobs Initiative (WTJI), National Social Economy Initiative, and others. Important impetus also came with the publication of the EU Commission's (1993) *White Paper on Growth, Competitiveness, and Employment* (which strongly endorsed the potential of the social economy) and the EU Operational Programme for Local Urban and Rural Development (1994-1999).

However, third sector organisations becoming increasingly dependent on such schemes also have encountered vulnerabilities due to short-term political expediency and economic contingency. State support of this kind is partly conditioned by a mix of political ideology and the wider boom-bust cycles of the global economy. For example, in 1999, the Minister for

8 The significant 'solidarity economy' in Italy, for example, has been linked to the historical strength of such ideologies, notably within the 19th century civic mutualism tradition, and Catholic solidarity values, which produced a widespread network of associations. Many of these evolved into social enterprises/co-operatives (Corbino, 2012).

Enterprise, Trade and Employment signalled the intention to cut back CE schemes, with the aim of reducing this support for local development on a phased basis over a five-year period. In 2003, it became apparent that the government intended to cut both the CE and WTJI schemes substantially and to withdraw support for the nascent Social Economy Programme.

Such moves showed how social economy policy is highly dependent on the broader economic environment. In the boom, the general reduction in unemployment and the service industry's need for a larger pool of low-paid workers was a factor behind cuts. In the very recent period of global crisis, with its particularly virulent manifestation in Ireland (O'Hanlon, 2010), austerity and fiscal conservatism with regard to social expenditure have left the sector even more vulnerable. For example, there have been cutbacks in allowances and training supports in the CE and WTJI schemes and funding for the Local and Community Development Programme.

At the same time, the new Tús scheme was introduced with the global impetus of IMF pressures for reforms. This is a community work placement scheme providing short-term placements for the unemployed. The work is targeted at needs in the community and as such it 'moves into' a space within the local development infrastructure. There are 5,000 places in Tús, and it brings significant pressure to bear on unemployed people to accept job offers on the scheme (including the threat of termination of social welfare payments). Positions on the scheme run for 12 months. There are considerable concerns about these pressures to participate and the short-term nature of the positions. The lifeblood of the community-voluntary sector is the spirit and energy that comes from voluntary enthusiasm and long-term (or indeed lifetime) commitment to the 'cause', whether that is the well-being of a local community or particular needs group, tackling an issue or set of issues, or seeking to contribute to social change or indeed wider societal transformation.

REFLECTIONS: CONTESTED ECONOMIC SPACES

The 'meaning' of any developmental dynamic – such as globalisation or the social economy – is always *produced* relationally through a long, difficult process of discourse, practice and engagement underpinned by an enduring tension between dominant and alternative meanings and values. Over recent decades, the Irish development model has been oriented to a considerable degree towards market strategies, transnational capital and consumerism. However, global processes of economic restructuring and the uneven effects across particular social and spatial sites created a context of inequality and marginalisation within which community and State actors (arguably driven by different imperatives and ideologies) turned to third sector or informal economic strategies to cope or to compensate.

However, there is significant divergence in economic philosophies across State and community-voluntary actors (though it would be wrong to imply in a simplistic way a clear consensus among community activists, who vary in their political commitment to or practical emphasis on service provision, training, equality, justice, social change agendas, etc). In particular, there may be a tension between a vision of a needs-based or people-centred development model or a vehicle for social change and a more modest or pragmatic view of social enterprise as a labour-market tool or a 'band-aid' for the hurt of poverty and marginalisation. The concern is that limiting State views of the sector as a temporary or secondary economic solution undermines the value of this work, resulting in constant pressures to move people into 'real' employment as soon as possible. In the latter vision, its primary function is to improve the market 'employability' of participant workers (Byrne *et al.*, 1999). Thus the social economy becomes a quick fix in difficult (global) times. The threat to funding in recent years is a simple practical manifestation of such a view, as is the pressure to participate and the time limit on participation in the Tús scheme. More widely, there remain concerns about the cultural meaning and value attached variously to paid/unpaid and formal/informal work in Irish society.

Nevertheless, the meaning of the social economy is still up for grabs in certain crucial respects, despite the intense difficulties of these current austere times. Some areas of alternative economic practice may well be incorporated as a plank in the broader neo-liberal scaffold of global capitalism – for example, as a labour-market tool or 'workfare'-style scheme. Other alternative economic spaces will continue to be mined productively and creatively, sometimes in surprising or challenging ways, part of development models constructed around the needs of daily life, not commodified, not externally controlled, not wholly alienating. However, we need a careful, critical awareness of how such alternatives always are affected by dominant ideologies and priorities, most obviously through dependence on State/governmental support. This relationship between the State and bottom-up actors is one characterised by uneven power relations and tendencies towards co-option on terms largely set by the dominant political economy. It is important analytically and politically to be realistic about these very real challenges to building a progressive alternative development model.

CONCLUSIONS

Overall, social enterprise can be located conceptually within a wider framework of alternative economic spaces. These are spaces of development populated by non-profit institutions (such as social enterprises, social economy initiatives, community organisations, households, etc.), which emphasise different imperatives and values to those of the dominant State-market sectors. Within the Irish context, the evolution of alternative economic activity of this kind has been shaped by wider patterns of economic restructuring, shifting tides in political ideologies and cultural changes, particularly with respect to community solidarity and individualism.

More specifically, the social economy has been given a noteworthy position within EU and Irish policy, particularly as a response to some of the inequalities of recent decades. In practice, as a result, third-sector organisations have been able to create a diverse infrastructure of needs-based development, but at the same time have become dependent on uncertain funding streams and vulnerable to short-term political expediency and economic contingency. This reveals a certain tension between a people-centred developmental vision at bottom-up level and a pragmatic view of social enterprise as a labour-market or anti-poverty tool at central level.

Alternative economic spaces have a long and important history and will continue to be pursued creatively and productively, but it is important to be critically aware of the real limits and challenges that exist in their relationship to the wider political economy and culture.

2 Social enterprise or social entrepreneurship: economic solidarity or market hegemony?

Deiric Ó Broin

INTRODUCTION

This chapter examines the contested terms 'social enterprise' and 'social entrepreneur', in particular the very different social, political and economic paradigms that each, this chapter contends, represents. The first section briefly examines the historical context in which this debate is taking place. The chapter then reviews the two distinct paradigms. The former is a broad approach to economic development based on economic and social solidarity and a more democratised society, the latter an evolution of the recent marketisation of the management and delivery of many public services. This is followed by an examination of the current discourse and the likely consequences for public policy in Ireland.

At this stage, it is important to note that many people use the terms 'social enterprise' and 'social entrepreneur' interchangeably. This can be problematic and there is a very definite vagueness inherent in much of the debate in Ireland. This chapter contends that there are a variety of very different and often mutually exclusive perspectives that require critical engagement. It is hoped that this chapter will contribute to the broader debate about the potential and actual nature and role of social enterprise and social entrepreneurs in Ireland.

THE HISTORICAL CONTEXT

For the purposes of this chapter, it is helpful to situate the current debate about social enterprise and social entrepreneurship in the context of the recent collapse of social partnership and the ongoing economic crises[9] facing certain models of capitalism in the Western world (Morgan, 2004: 1). In doing so, the chapter aims to examine the current lack of a broadly accepted model of public deliberation and economic management in Ireland and to briefly note that not all models of capitalism in the West are facing the same issues as Ireland and the majority of issues arising from the current crises are manifesting in many different ways in many different countries. In a number of cases, the crises are barely figuring – for example, in Australia.

The social partnership process evokes a very significant level of rhetoric and academic interest and yet, for many, its impact remains unclear. Was it a constructive factor in 'creating the new and vibrant Ireland of today?' (Hastings *et al.*, 2007: ix). If so, despite certain efforts at inclusive dialogue, has it also had a concurrent negative impact on the nature of democratic

10 The chapter uses the term 'crises' rather than 'crisis' because of the multi-stranded and separate nature of the economic, political and regulatory challenges facing Ireland.

deliberation in Ireland? It is important to discuss why social partnership seemed to receive a warm embrace from so many stake-holders involved in public policy. Why was social partnership accepted so readily and are there ramifications for the social enterprise/social entrepreneur debate?

Three distinct, though related, reasons stand out as to why the Irish political system and its many stakeholders "embraced the social partnership model so passionately:

- The economic circumstances of the 1980s;
- The existence of a political and institutional culture that was sympathetic to corporatist/neo-corporatist solutions;
- The resilience of the existing state apparatus"[10] (Ó Broin, 2009: 114).

It is also important to note that, while there was opposition to social partnership, including from government backbenchers, some free-market think tanks and a small number of academics,[11] by and large enough interest groups were satisfied with its method of operation to ensure its continuing success. The calamity facing the Irish economy in the 1980s is widely understood at this stage and the fact that it helped to initiate a new form of public governance is accepted by the majority of political scientists. What is interesting is that Ireland did not follow the neo-liberal route chosen by many other countries in the Anglo-American sphere.

The current situation is very interesting for those involved in the debate about the potential nature and role of social enterprise and social entrepreneurs. Despite the resilience of many of the institutions of social partnership to previous upheavals (for example, the National Economic and Social Council), the scale and multi-stranded nature of the current crisis has been fatal. The institutional framework of social partnership[12] is in what could be best described as a state of flux. Some of the outlines of a new model

---

10 One of the very interesting aspects of the social partnership era was the lack of substantive institutional reform of the State. There was a very significant expansion in the number of agencies (Clancy and Murphy, 2006; Ó Broin and Watters, 2007) but less visible reform of existing institutions and processes. By and large, swathes of the State's institutions remained unreformed and retained their identity and ability to shape public policy outcomes.

11 Politicians such Noel Ahern TD, thinks tanks such as the Open Republic Institute and academics including Seamus Ó Cinnéide. See Ó Broin (2009: 118-121) for a more detailed analysis of the Irish critiques of social partnership.

12 For example the National Economic and Social Council and the continuation of regular and structured meetings between ICTU, IBEC, IFA and government.

of public deliberation and economic governance[13] can be dimly perceived but there remains a great deal of 'institutional space' in which to innovate. It is this 'institutional space' and this transitional moment that makes the decisions about the potential nature and role of social enterprise and social entrepreneurs so important – for example, an expansion of the delivery of existing services by locally-accountable social enterprises and using public procurement as a tool to enhance local economies (Doyle and Lalor, 2010).

BUILDING A MODEL OF ECONOMIC SOLIDARITY

The chapter contends that implementing a model of greater economic and social solidarity is a distinct possibility at this moment. As Amin observes: "governments around the world, supported by parties and institutions of varying political hue, have begun to introduce legislation and policies to stimulate and support the social economy" (2009: 5). This change is linked to the ongoing crisis in the current model of capitalism but also stems from a "desire to make capitalism more caring through markets and modes of delivery that are socially-responsible, needs-based and stakeholder-oriented" (*ibid.*). In this context, a number of relevant conceptual frameworks can contribute to an understanding of the potential characteristics of a society based on more robust economic and social solidarity. For the purposes of this chapter, the broad perspective of 'associationalism', also known as 'associative democracy', is used.[14] This perspective argues that the involvement of participant-led and accountable associations in economic activities normally undertaken by the State or large companies offers great opportunities to develop more sustainable economies and more accountable democracies.

While many political theorists view the type and scale of devolution of political power proposed by associative or associational theorists as utopian, associationalists regard it as the way to invigorate democracy generally, both

[13] These include changes at national level, like the establishment of the Irish Fiscal Advisory Council, the Government's Economic Management Council, and proposed changes at local level, which include a series of councillor-centred reforms of the Irish local government and local development systems and the establishment of a more coherent and structured enterprise system linked to a reformed local government system. One also could include a new openness to social enterprises playing an enhanced role in local economies.

[14] In particular the writings of Paul Hirst (1989, 1994, 1995 and 1997) and the more recent work of Joshua Cohen and Joel Rogers (1995) on the central role allocated to social enterprises or associations.

in large-scale political societies and in local institutions.[15] Warren (2001: 3) notes that "within democratic theory a remarkable consensus is emerging around Tocqueville's view that the virtue and viability of a democracy depend on the robustness of its associational life" – that is, community-based organisations, chambers of commerce, representative groups and other civil society organisations.[16] The proponents of associationalism claim that it can provide the "social substance of liberal democratic procedures, underwrite the very possibility of markets and provide the means of resistance and alternatives when states or markets fail" (Warren, 2001: 4). This a key issue for supporters of social enterprises; associationalists argue that such associations provide a form of critical 'soft' infrastructure that underpins our communities and broader society. Without this infrastructure, society is weakened and collective solutions to collective problems are difficult to agree and operationalise.

In *Associative Democracy: New Forms of Economic and Social Governance*, Hirst outlines a model of associationalism based on the contention that there is a "deep and widespread dissatisfaction about both economic performance and the health of democracy" (Hirst, 1993: 116).[17] He is adamant that recent experiences have heightened awareness of the lack of citizen control over decision-makers. For Hirst, associationalism is premised on three basic principles of political organisation:

- That voluntary self-governing associations should be the primary means of democratic governance;
- That power should be decentralised to the lowest level consistent with the effective governance of social and economic matters – that "the principles of state pluralism and federation should prevail" (Hirst, 1994: 20); and
- That there should be a continuous flow of information between governors and the governed.

---

15 The terms associative and associational are used interchangeably as are associationalism and associative democracy.

16 Robert Putnam's recent writings on social capital have been particularly influential in initiating and developing this 'consensus' – in particular, *Making Democracy Work: Civic Traditions in Modern Italy* (1993) and *Bowling Alone – The Collapse and Revival of American Community* (2000). An interesting example of this pervasive influence can be seen in the NESF report *The Policy Implications of Social Capital in Ireland* (Forum Report No. 26) – in particular, the document's mapping of the relationship between community development and social capital.

17 Hirst's work draws upon the earlier work of British social theorists such as G.D.H. Cole, Harold Laski and J.N. Figgis and mutualist writers such as Pierre-Joseph Proudhon.

Cohen and Rogers (1995) outline a related perspective that aims to show how strengthening the discretionary powers of local, voluntary and self-governing associations would enhance the way that modern democracies function by facilitating "informed legitimate state policies and promoting social justice" (Cunningham, 2002: 137).

Associationalism as outlined by Hirst and Cohen and Rogers differs in a number of minor respects. The role of the State in each variant is of importance. Cohen and Rogers emphasise that they do not favour dismantling the central State or advocate a minimal State in the manner of neo-liberalism.[18] In addition, they note that the State is needed for tasks of society-wide co-ordination or for meeting needs that no voluntary associations exist to serve. Despite his concerns regarding the potentially stifling role of the State, Hirst also represents associative democracy not as an exclusive alternative but as a "supplement and healthy competitor" to what he sees as the "current dominant forms of social organisation: representative mass democracy, bureaucratic state welfare and the big corporation" (1994: 42).

This chapter contends that associationalism has two significant contributions to make to the current debate about the potential nature and role of social enterprise and social entrepreneurs. The first of these is its focus on the representation of the "unorganised and underorganised", in particular the suggestion that "associative resources" should be provided to labour and other non-business groups to enable them to engage on a more equal footing to address the "overwhelming business dominance" of most modern States (Cohen and Rogers, 1995: 78). This is a critical insight and will be discussed in more detail later in the chapter. The second contribution is related to the first, in that it proposes a form of "bargaining" between social partners, designed to address the domination of bargaining arenas by local business interests (*ibid.*). Again, the focus on providing an equitable base for all social groups is important and will be examined later in this chapter.

In this model, social enterprises could be key components of a reinvigorated and empowered society and not passive recipients of State largesse and philanthropic goodwill. As democratically-owned and accountable economic entities, they would act as locally-empowering organisations, and not merely service deliverers, but also represent a new

---

18 They give examples of devising, interpreting and administering polices regarding environmental standards, occupational health and safety, vocational training and consumer protection. However, these must conform to certain standards, including openness of membership, internal democracy, budgetary transparency and the prohibition of such things as violence, racism or criminal behaviour.

approach to economic and social governance. Such an approach rooted in solidarity and subsidiarity is likely also to lead to other benefits – for example, *The Spirit Level – Why Equality is Better for Everyone* explains that communities oriented towards co-operative or social economy models of economic activity tend to be healthier and suffer less from a variety of illnesses (Wilkinson and Pickett, 2009: 260).

MARKET-ORIENTED SOCIAL INNOVATION

In its edition of 14 August 2010, *The Economist* included a very insightful piece on governments' interest in what it termed 'social innovation' and the role of social entrepreneurs. Central to the article was the observation that social innovation "differs from the fashion of the past couple of decades for contracting out the delivery of public services to businesses and non-profit groups in order to cut costs, in that it aims to do more than save a few dollars or pounds – although this is part of the attraction. The idea is to transform the way public services are provided, by tapping into the ingenuity of people in the private sector, especially social entrepreneurs" (2010: 51). Social entrepreneurs develop "innovative answers to a social problem" (*ibid.*). It is suggested that the fresh, businesslike ideas of social entrepreneurs will bring about the productivity miracle in the "social sector", defined as the public sector plus service-delivering charities, similar to the one that began in businesses in the 1990s. Muhammad Yunus, founder of Grameen, and Wendy Kopp, founder of Teach for America, are portrayed as representatives of this new approach. Edwards used the term 'philanthrocapitalism' to describe a similar, though not synonymous, process of applying business principles to the world of civil society and noted that this process had "fashion, wealth, power and celebrity behind it" (2009: 11). He described the Bill and Melinda Gates Foundation and the Clinton Global Initiative as good examples of this approach to social progress. LaMarche contends that what separates these newer social entrepreneurs or philanthrocapitalists from the likes of Carnegie is "their emphasis on measurability, on incorporating lessons from the business world" (2009: 23). *Philanthrocapitalism – How The Rich Can Save the World and Why We Should Let Them* adds another characteristic, the harnessing of the "profit motive to achieve social good" (Bishop and Green, 2008: 6).

This brief outline above may appear limited and rather unfair in comparison to the treatment of associationalism but it raises a key issue about social entrepreneurs – that is, there is very little analysis. A number are known and promoted, the underpinning rationales (the application of business-linked knowledge and principles and the profit motive) appear to be widely accepted but it is difficult to ascertain a publicly articulated philosophy of action. Bishop and Green (2008) note Bono's support for social entrepreneurs but this chapter suggests that it is not enough to state that social entrepreneurs are innovators who establish, lead, manage or work in social enterprises. There is more to it. Not all innovators in the social economy consider themselves social entrepreneurs because of the market-linked connotations. Many innovators in the social economy, managing and leading social enterprises, are addressing market failures and their consequences.

QUESTIONING THE ROLE OF SOCIAL ENTERPRISE AND SOCIAL ENTREPRENEURS

An objective of this chapter is to contribute to an ongoing debate in the broad social economy, in which both social enterprises and social entrepreneurs operate, particularly as the current political and economic environment appears to be conducive to a major reconfiguring of Irish economic activity in favour of the social economy. As noted earlier, Amin's description of a more caring and distributive model of capitalism seems quite possible and the potential may exist for a model of Irish capitalism that is rooted in our societal development and experience and within the framework of more distributive northern European model of capitalism.

However, a concern, and this is written as an academic political scientist with a personal interest in the area rather than expertise, is that it is unclear what the many actors in the Irish social economy are striving for. Is there a shared vision? Given the different origins, backgrounds and objectives of the many organisations and individuals, is such a suggestion even possible? The confusing jumble of terms – for example, social innovation, social economy, social enterprise, community and voluntary sectors, social entrepreneurs, etc. – is striking. The fact that each term has a different meaning to different people is equally telling and clearly indicates not only the lack of a shared vision but also the absence of a shared vocabulary.

In this context, it is helpful to discuss 'developmental' and 'instrumental' perspectives on social enterprise and social entrepreneurs. From the developmental perspective, there is an intrinsic and empowering value in the establishment of social enterprises. Associationalist thinkers outline a compelling vision of a radically decentralised, empowered and fluid society with robust economic solidarity. From the instrumental perspective (as a means to another end – and it appears that some in the Irish government share this perspective), it is the efficiency gains that flow from the application of business principles by social entrepreneurs that make social enterprises useful or worthwhile. By delivering certain services cheaper and more effectively, they serve an important purpose.

Neither of these perspectives is to be condemned or lauded, they are rooted in different places, but they are different. That difference is worth observing and engaging with. It will be only one of many but it is important to what happens in the coming years. Edwards warns that the social economy "needs different organising principles from business because it has different goals" (2009: 9). That does not mean inefficiency is somehow inherent to the social economy. It just means it is different and sometimes that is forgotten.

CONCLUSIONS

In most European States, democratisation and the rise of the modern welfare state provided the foundation for "unprecedented improvements in the material conditions of the bulk of society, and greater room for the actualisation of individuals' skills, aptitudes and talents" (Wood and Roper, 2004: 253). Ireland had a rather unusual trajectory, at least in relation to other EU Member States, and social enterprises have played a very significant role in our societal development – for example, Raiffeisen Banks,[19]Approved Local Councils,[20] credit unions and agricultural co-operatives – and the current economic crises have provided an opportunity for many to question the role of the State in providing certain services. That is fair and appropriate. It is not necessarily regressive and does not amount to an attack on the 'public sphere'. It is possible to envision an alternative model development – for example, associationalism – that is empowering, committed to social justice and a redistributive capitalism and not wedded to what Cole called the "omnicompetent State" (1920).

However, the language employed by many writers about social entrepreneurs and by social entrepreneurs themselves is problematic. It appears to take for granted that the State, and for that matter any form of co-ordinated public action, is inherently inefficient and needs to be marketised – that somehow the application of business processes will address complex social and economic problems. The consequences of this ideological action

---

19 Raiffeisen Banks operated in Ireland from the 1890s until the early 1930s (Colvin and McLoughlin, 2012).

20 Approved Local Councils operated in a number of Irish communities in the 1940s and 1950s and delivered services on behalf of county councils (Gallagher, 2000).

remain largely unquestioned. Why? Given the transitional period Ireland is currently living through, and the variety of possibilities for the provision of social and infrastructural services on offer, there is a danger that an approach to the social economy may be adopted and implemented by the Irish State that is socially unsustainable, - that is, rather than invest in the social and community infrastructure necessary to develop and sustain social enterprises, there may be a trend to outsource the delivery of services to community-based organisations that are not equipped to manage an significant increase in turnover.

It is both essential and feasible to embed the social economy as a key component of a new model of economic development in Ireland and this process has to be embedded in a robust series of discussions about the role and nature of social enterprises and social entrepreneurs, how they see themselves, how others perceive them and how a consensus might be developed. At this stage in the Ireland's social and economic development, it is vital we avoid what Unger refers to as the "dictatorship of no alternatives" (2009: 1).

3 Social enterprise and the green economy

Gerard Doyle

INTRODUCTION

Getting clarity on the meaning of the green economy is difficult, as it is an ideological concept. For proponents of a free market economy, it can constitute a wide array of goods and services, including renewable energy, waste management, and water treatment that – if developed – could contribute to the economic renewal of the Irish economy resulting in the generation of a new source of employment (Forfás, 2009).

For others, the green economy also can be defined as a sustainable economy where all energy is derived from renewable resources, which are naturally replenished.[21] Proponents of a sustainable model of the green economy are not just concerned with economic development but also with how economic activity is conducted.

Lander (2011) asserts that the concept of a green economy (as defined by the United Nations Environment Programme[22]) is ultimately flawed because he believes that environmental sustainability cannot be achieved while pursuing economic growth.

To address what Lander sees as the fundamental incompatibility between economic growth and environmental sustainability, Jackson (2011) believes that there is an urgent need among governments throughout the world to transform their economic models. He advocates a new system where the culture of consumerism is dismantled, and where ecological economics are adopted – this would see a shift to low-carbon, labour-intensive activities, tight regulation of financial markets, and investment in ecological jobs that reduce energy consumption. However, such a transformation will not occur unless there is a change in the culture and norms of a society.

The third sector and community initiatives that are mushrooming throughout the developed and developing world should be supported by their respective governments to contribute to community resilience and autonomy, according to Jackson (2011). Indeed, Wilkinson and Pickett (2009) state that social enterprises, and specifically co-operatives, could play a central role in the creation of a more equal society.

It is in this context that social enterprise will be examined to assess its role in Ireland in developing a new economic model, which is significantly less demanding on the earth's resources and, in particular, is less reliant on fossil fuels, is more resource-efficient and provides a template for a more

---

21 www. greeneconomygroup.com

22 The mandate of the United Nations Environmental Programme (UNEP) is to be the leading global environmental authority. It has six main areas of work: climate change, disasters and conflicts, ecosystem management, environmental governance, harmful substances and resource efficiency.

egalitarian form of enterprise. This new economic model would be supportive of self-reliant communities that can exert greater levels of economic self-determination. Amin *et al.* (2002: 125) state that social enterprise protagonists "see what they do as advocacy as another way of life; one based on social commitment, ethical/ environmental citizenship and as a vehicle for self and social enhancement". Pearce (1993) asserts that a core mission of many social enterprises is meeting needs for their communities while not having an adverse impact on their community's environment.

THE RATIONALE FOR RENEWABLE ENERGY

The rationale for co-operative renewable energy is that co-operatives:

- Can play an important role in increasing public acceptance of renewable energy, particularly wind energy (Walker *et al.*, 2007) because the benefits to communities are visible;
- Can play an active role in educating the public about renewable energy (Walker *et al.*, 2007);
- Are an effective mechanism for generating employment and for rural regeneration (Barry and Chapman, 2009);
- Reduce leakages from a local economy, generating a greater multiplier effect (New Economics Foundation, 2002).

In 2008, Ireland imported 89% of its total energy consumption (SEAI, 2010). In 2007, the EU agreed new energy targets: a 20% reduction in greenhouse gases by 2020; 20% energy efficiency by 2020[23] and 20% of the EU energy consumption to be from renewable sources based on 1990 levels (DCENR, 2010). *Directive 2009/28/EC* sets a binding individual target for each Member State, which contribute to the achievement of the overall EU goal. Each Member State has a number of sectors across which to reach the targets, namely heat, transport and electricity. Aside from reducing transport energy by 10%, each government has flexibility in how it attains its targets. Ireland's overall target is to generate 16% of all its energy from renewable sources – if these targets are not met, Ireland can be sanctioned by the EU.

---

23 The EU is aiming for a 20% cut in Europe's annual primary energy consumption by 2020. The Commission has proposed several measures to increase efficiency at all stages of the energy chain: generation, transformation, distribution and final consumption. The measures focus on public transport and the building sector, where the potential for savings is greatest. Other measures include the introduction of smart meters (which encourage consumers to manage their energy use better), and clearer product labelling sourced from http://ec.europa.eu/energy/ efficiency/index_en.htm.

Although energy from renewable sources currently comprises only a small percentage of total energy consumption, Ireland has abundant natural resources suitable for renewable energy (Feasta, 2007). Indeed, communities have ample opportunities to exploit renewable energy resources in the form of biomass, wind and solar. However, for many communities experiencing economic marginalisation, this will require State support.

COMMUNITY RENEWABLE ENERGY IN DENMARK

Ireland can learn a lot from Denmark in how communities there have embraced renewable energy through social enterprise development (in the form of co-operatives). In so doing, they have fortified their local economies and strengthened community self-reliance.

Wind power

A high proportion of Denmark's wind power capacity is owned by co-operatives or guilds. In 2002, 5,600 wind turbines, which equated to 23% of Denmark's wind capacity in that year, were owned by co-operatives (Bolinger, 2001).[24] A key factor in the growth of co-operatives was the formation of the Danish Association of Wind Power Guilds (DV), a non-profit, independent association of wind farm co-operatives, responsible for representing the co-operatives' interests with respect to local authorities, utilities and wind-turbine manufacturers. However, at the beginning of this century, co-operatives were being offered substantial amounts of money to sell their windmills. Investors then traded these windmills for the right to erect larger ones. As a result in 2009, there were 50,000 people who co-owned windmills, down from 150,000 at the start of the century (Maegard, 2009).

The process for initiating wind farms generally entails these steps:

- A local person has the idea for a wind farm;
- She/he gets the assistance of a few other residents;
- They find a small number of farmers living in close proximity willing to erect turbines on their farms;

24 Bolinger (2001) states that, due to ownership restrictions in Denmark, joint ownership of wind turbines in Denmark has taken the form of general partnership /full liability company rather that of a co-operative. This chapter adopts a broad understanding of ownership models, encompassing different forms of collective citizen-based ownership of energy-generating facilities, which are not necessarily in the legal form of a co-operative.

- They gain community support for the initiative at a series of public meetings;
- They join DV, which provides advice on legal issues and assists with the formation of the co-operative.

DV has played an important role in advocating for a benign environment for the growth of the co-operative sector in wind energy. However, as wind power developed in Denmark, smaller community and farmer-owned (on-shore) wind farms have not become owners of larger off-shore wind farms, resulting in communities losing out to corporate entities. Nonetheless, the co-operative wind sector has facilitated acceptance of wind energy as communities directly benefit from it. The benefits include economic development of rural communities.

District heating systems

In addition to wind power, co-operatives play a central role in the operation of district heating systems[25] outside of Denmark's major cities. As a result of the *Heat Supply Act, 1979*,[26] local authorities were obliged to formulate heating plans. This stimulated major investment in heating networks, and local authorities were mandated to make consumers connect to new district heating systems.[27] However, to counterbalance being compelled to switch to district heating systems, consumer co-operatives were formed to manage them thus ensuring consumer control. As they are not-for-profit operations, heating costs were kept to a minimum: heating costs were calculated to cover costs only, prices are set annually, and any surplus is re-invested in improving the district heating system or in reducing prices. Furthermore, due to their democratic structures, members of the district heating system have an input into running of the operation.

This process of switching to district heating systems took two decades to implement.

---

25 A district heating system works like a domestic central heating system only on a larger scale. Water is heated using a boiler located in a central heating plant. The heat is distributed to the customer *via* an underground network of insulated pipes. The water in the network is continually circulating and therefore is always available to the householder.

26 The *Heat Supply Act, 1979*, stipulated there would be municipal heat supply planning in each municipality, a new natural gas infrastructure, a substantial increase in district heating, and that district heating would shift from fossil fuel boilers to combined heat and power plants and renewable energy.

27 The rationale for establishing district heating systems was to make Denmark less reliant on fossil fuels.

COMMUNITY RENEWABLE ENERGY IN SCOTLAND

The Scottish Government intends to generate 40% of its renewable energy from renewable sources. To this end, in 2011, it established the Community and Renewable Energy Scheme (CARES), which provides loan finance to communities that intend to establish community-owned renewable energy projects. The CARES loan fund aims to provide loans towards the high risk, pre-planning consent stages of renewable energy projects. The scheme is managed on behalf of Scottish Ministers by Community Energy Scotland Ltd. A key feature of the scheme is that security is not required on the loan finance. The Scottish Government recognises that community-owned renewable energy can provide a range of benefits in addition to securing source of energy, and it intends to achieve 500 megawatts of community and locally-owned renewable energy by 2020.[28]

Another key feature of Scotland's drive to support renewable energy social enterprise is that communities can avail of expertise from Community Energy Scotland.[29]

The Scottish Government has been supportive of communities engaging in renewable energy. The following two case studies demonstrate what can be achieved by community organisations initiating the move away from fossil fuel consumption and embracing social enterprise development.

> Knoydart is a small community in the Scottish Highlands that uses hydro power to provide electricity to all of its properties *via* a small local grid. The plant was developed to preserve the Knoydart environment and to provide cost-effective, clean and efficient electricity to the local community. The project is owned by the Knoydart Foundation.[30] The hydro plan provides the community with all its electricity and the surplus power generates an income which covers the maintenance of the hydro facility. The bulk of the capital was secured from the European Regional Development Fund (ERDF) and from the community's own reserves (Hoggett, 2000).

---

28 http://www.communityenergyscotland.org.uk/support/cares.

29 Community Energy Scotland (CES) is a membership-based organisation, whose members can share knowledge and connect to other member groups that are developing, or who have already developed, community energy projects. CES provides detailed, independent and ongoing support for all aspects of community energy project development, from micro to megawatt scale.

30 The Knoydart Foundation was established in 1997 to work on behalf of the community in taking ownership of the area of land covered by the Knoydart estate (www.knoydart-foundation.com).

The Isle of Eigg is one of the small Isles in the Scottish Inner Hebrides. After decades of problems with absentee landlords in the 20th century, the island was bought in 1997 by the Isle of Eigg Heritage Trust, a partnership between the residents of Eigg, the Highland Council, and the Scottish Wildlife Trust (Mcintosh, 2001).

After upgrading the pier, building a café and other buildings to accommodate tourists visiting the island in the summer months, the Heritage Trust decided to derive its energy from renewable sources rather than from imported fossil fuels.

An independent electricity grid, which makes continuous power available to all 86 residents and the small number of businesses on the island, has enabled the island to become energy self-sufficient. The new grid is supplied by three hydro generators, four wind turbines and solar photovoltaic panels. When renewable energy sources are generating surplus energy, power is conserved in batteries or used to heat communal buildings. In the event of the grid needing a boost in energy, there are diesel generators – however, these are rarely required.

Renewable power meets up to 95% of the island's energy requirement because people are careful with what they use. Each domestic property can use 5kW at any one time (enough for an electric kettle and washing machine to run simultaneously) and every dwelling has an energy monitor which informs the household if they are approaching the energy threshold. Further, home insulation initiatives have led to reduction in energy consumption.

In addition to renewable energy, the island's population has changed their lifestyles in many ways in the drive to become more self-sufficient. In particular, many residents are growing more of their own food, so less needs to be brought in from the mainland. They compost, reuse, recycle, and exchange unwanted items. Residents take as many trips as possible by bicycle or on foot, and in winter the community has access to a bus which is run on waste cooking oil from the ferry.

The island is planning to use prize money gained from being a finalist in a national competition to deploy an anaerobic digestor,[31] and to

31 Anaerobic digestion means without air and it entails a complex biochemical transformation that extracts energy as biogas from organic waste *via* an anaerobic digestor (an airless warmed sealed container). Moreover, anaerobic digestion produces a useful solid that can be segregated into fibre and liquor serving as a conditioner and

purchase electric vehicles for residents to lease.[32] The drive for renewable energy has provided economic opportunities for islanders and employment and this has contributed to young people returning to the Island.[33]

COMMUNITY RENEWABLE ENERGY IN IRELAND

In Ireland, there are over 30 community renewable energy projects that are either operational or at planning stage. Many of them will be incorporated as community co-operatives or as forms of social enterprises (Comhar and TCD, 2011).

One such social enterprise was established by Fuinneamh Glas Teoranta, Inis Meáin, the Aran Islands, as a cooperative in 2002. The power generated from three wind turbines is used in a desalination plant for potable water and the excess energy is sold into the grid. The necessary capital was secured from the EU, Údarás na Gaeltachta, Galway County Council and the Island Co-operative on Inis Meáin (Comhar and TCD, 2011).

Another renewable social enterprise is Camphill Ballytobin, part of Camphill Communities of Ireland, which works with people with intellectual disabilities. It provides accommodation to 85 people and includes a primary school, workshops and a community hall. Since 1999, the community has used biogas (produced from an anaerobic digestion plant) to supply heat to houses and the other buildings on the site. The anaerobic digestion plant collects agricultural waste from local farmers and delivers treated nutrient-rich soil back to the farmers. The project displaces at least 380 tonnes of carbon dioxide per year. Profits are reinvested back into the community to fund buildings and equipment (Comhar and TCD, 2011).

Local Switch is a social enterprise model being promoted by two of the founders of the Cloughjordan Eco Village. The business model will see the Local Switch co-operative working with interested communities throughout the State in developing social enterprises to produce renewable energy district heating systems. The community benefits from this model through

fertilizer respectively. These two products have lower pollution potential than slurries for plant growing.

32 Islanders on Eigg in the Hebrides have won £300,000 in the National Endowment for Science, Technology and the Arts' Big Green Challenge to spend on community projects that reduce CO_2 emissions. In 2009, the Eigg team reduced CO_2 emissions by 32%. The UK's 2020 emissions reduction target is 34%.

33 www.islandgogreen.org (accessed in March 2012).

participating households and businesses having reduced energy bills and ownership of the renewable energy system. The members of the social enterprise will gain a return on their investment in the form of an annual dividend or alternatively decide to collectively invest the surplus income to establish other social enterprises.

CONCLUSIONS

The experiences of Denmark and Scotland demonstrate the central role social enterprises and co-operatives could play in Ireland's switch from a fossil fuel-dependent economy to one where communities have greater control in supplying their own energy from renewable sources. A number of communities in Ireland have already become aware of the benefits of generating their own heat and electricity.

New partnerships can be formed between communities and other parties, including third level institutions, which are developing new technologies in this area.

State support through a combination of loan and grant finance would ensure that more marginalised communities have capital to develop community renewable energy systems and, in so doing, would reduce the incidence of fuel poverty in their respective communities. Finance could be provided through the National Pension Reserve. Indeed, such an investment would contribute in a small way to a number of Ireland's policy goals being achieved.

Perhaps the most important outcome of community engagement in renewable energy would be for citizens to become aware of the benefits of more ecologically-grounded economic activity. Over time, communities could collectively campaign for the State to support them to have greater control over Ireland's natural resources and for such resources to be harnessed to produce clean renewable energy for the benefit of all Irish citizens and future generations rather than indigenous and foreign corporate interests. Although social enterprises and co-operatives can play an important role in the transformation to a sustainable economy, it will require a grass roots movement to struggle for a new economic system and society that fundamentally rejects our current economic model predicated on infinite economic growth.

4 Support for social enterprises

Tom Daly, Gerard Doyle and Tanya Lalor

INTRODUCTION

Compared to a number of EU States, the Irish State to date has viewed social enterprise as performing a marginal and residual role in Irish economic development. This is evidenced by the narrow range of policies and supports dedicated to social enterprise compared to conventional enterprise development. The State's primary policy intervention was the establishment of State-funded programmes that support community organisations which employ social groups that are at a distance from the labour market (Molloy *et al.*, 2000).

This chapter has a number of aims: first, it seeks to demonstrate that social enterprises encounter a number of barriers not experienced by private enterprises. This – and the fact that social enterprises have a combination of social and economic objectives – requires a dedicated and specialised support system. The effective development of social enterprises must be preceded by community development activity – otherwise, social enterprises will not develop decision-making structures that are participatory. The chapter will then detail the key features of a support structure.

THE BARRIERS TO SOCIAL ENTERPRISE DEVELOPMENT

Social enterprises encounter a number of constraints that adversely affect their prevalence and effectiveness (Smallbone *et al.*, 2001). Constraints external to disadvantaged communities include:

- Difficulties for social enterprise in entering the mainstream of economic policy, as the dominant economic model is underpinned by values that are not consistent with those of social enterprise. This is evidenced by the lack of national policy around social enterprise;
- Lack of appropriate finance, both grant and loan, for social enterprises at various stages of development (Bank of England, 2003);
- Central Government and State agencies' policies, practices and attitudes towards social enterprises (Chapman *et al.*, 2007). The lack of supports allocated to social enterprises compared to those afforded to private enterprises makes it difficult for them to grow, and reducing or withdrawing State funding from regeneration programmes prematurely can have an adverse impact on communities' efforts to develop social enterprises;

- The dearth of research on social enterprise within urban areas, preventing the gathering of evidence to support demands for additional resources for social enterprise interventions in disadvantaged communities.

Furthermore, other constraints within disadvantaged communities include:

- The absence of social enterprise activists with the necessary skills to grow social enterprises, including human resource expertise (Smallbone *et al.*, 2001) and in developing marketing strategies (Shaw, 2004);
- The demographics and extent of poverty in disadvantaged communities, which can make it difficult for social enterprises to access skilled labour and management expertise (Amin, 2005);
- The strategy of solely meeting an identified social need (for example, childcare or services to the elderly) rather than those with an economic focus, such as acquiring property and other assets for community benefit. This can limit the capacity of social enterprises to economically regenerate disadvantaged communities.

THE TYPES OF SUPPORTS REQUIRED

Daly (1998) has indicated that social enterprises require the following supports to address the barriers identified above:

- Provision of intensive support to community organisations and groups planning to develop social enterprises;
- Access to technical and professional expertise;
- Access to appropriate types of finance.

Time scale for support of social enterprise development

The timescale for support of social economy enterprises is usually long, and support needs to be provided from idea stage through to and, in many cases, beyond trading. Some of the reasons for long-term support include:

- The first three years are the most crucial in terms of the survival and development of an enterprise. For a social economy enterprise, many of which are operating in new markets, or creating new markets, maintained support in the early trading phase is important;
- Specific technical and enterprise expertise may be required;
- Training – formal and informal – including training on topics such as governance, accountability, and business planning.
- As trading develops, there is a need to ensure that the activities of the project are consistent with its aims and objectives. In some cases, aims and

objectives need to be re-evaluated in light of sustainability requirements and needs.

There is a rule of thumb within social enterprise development that the withdrawal from project support should take place gradually, over the first three years of trading or operation of a project. The focus of attention changes as a project starts to trade, and the emphasis during this phase is generally placed on monitoring financial performance, to ensure that overtrading does not occur.

Case example: The Social Economy Unit

Ireland's first (and, to date, only) dedicated support structure for social enterprises, the Social Economy Unit, was established in 1997 as a Tallaght Partnership[34] initiative and located within Get Tallaght Working,[35] a community co-operative providing enterprise development supports.

The Social Economy Unit was supported by the South Dublin EU URBAN initiative, the FÁS Community Enterprise Programme, the Tallaght Partnership and Get Tallaght Working.

The unit worked with a range of projects, including market-oriented social enterprises, local service delivery-oriented social enterprises, and worker co-ops. Criteria for support were that the projects were located in the social economy, were aimed at tackling disadvantage, and did not already have a support structure available to them.

The methodology of the unit was characterised by the provision of close project support to projects, from idea stage[36] to trading (and beyond, in some cases). The unit employed social economy advisors who worked closely with projects, sometimes taking on the role of interim project manager, when required. The unit facilitated the development of an enterprise management team, which undertook the operational tasks for the project, and which reported to the governance structures of the project.

The unit, during the development phase, worked with an enterprise focus but under the overall context and subordination of a separate community development working group. Social economy development work was undertaken only where there was a clear community benefit identified.

---

34 Now Dodder Valley Partnership.

35 Now Partas.

36 Where required.

THE DELIVERY OF SUPPORTS

As social enterprises require a particular type of support, the question arises as to how this type of support should be delivered.

There is consistent research evidence to suggest that mainstream support agencies have difficulties in understanding the concept of social enterprise and the principles on which they are predicated (HM Treasury, 1999). Lyon and Ramsden (2006) assert that social enterprises value the support and expertise gained from other social enterprises in their locality. A UK policy paper has recommended that policy-makers need to understand the relevance of social enterprise-specific support and how it can be incorporated into policy frameworks (WAG, 2003).

However, it is argued that State agencies are unlikely to be equipped with the resources or skills sets to deliver the supports required by social enterprises. There are a number of reasons for this.

First, there is limited understanding of social enterprises and their mission, values and *modus operandi*, even within the third sector itself.

Second, social enterprises are not passive recipients of support, but typically engage in a developmental process that includes community development as well as enterprise development. The balance between the two presents particular challenges to community organisations and requires an approach drawn from a community development approach with an understanding of enterprise (Daly, 1998). This has been the practice in innovative support structures for social enterprise in Ireland, such as the Social Economy Unit, highlighted above.

Third, a support structure may need to engage in lobbying work with social enterprises, and may test boundaries or extend beyond existing criteria for supports – this is most likely to be beyond the scope of traditional enterprise agencies. Social enterprises typically test new and innovative approaches to existing problems – and often can fall outside and challenge traditional concepts of viability and enterprise development.

Finally, a social enterprise support structure should be pro-active in identifying opportunities for social enterprise development, rather than simply responding to requests for support. It should have its own enterprise development and promotion function. Such a role is not within the remit of the State enterprise support apparatus.

For these reasons, an independent support structure that can provide project development support at local level, while lobbying for, and promoting, the sector and raising-awareness at national level is required. Such support structures should be located within the social economy itself. This is the practice across Europe where social enterprises and social co-operatives have successfully developed.[37] The absence of such an independent social enterprise support structure in Ireland makes it more difficult for many of the aforementioned barriers to be addressed.

This does not imply that the State has no role in social enterprise development – the implications for the State are outlined in a later section.

THE ROLE OF A LOCAL SUPPORT STRUCTURE

As stated above, a support structure should be located within the social economy. Such a structure should be accountable to the local community, to ensure its consistency with the projects that it actively supports. Its role would be to establish local strategies and action plans for supporting social enterprise. It should include the involvement of community representatives and activists in its governance structure.

Provide close project support

A support structure should employ social enterprise workers to assist community organisations to develop social enterprises, or indeed to identify a group that will pursue existing social enterprise opportunities. A policy should be developed to support a combination of different types of social enterprise – those with a market place orientation; local service provision orientation; member-controlled business – for member benefit as well as trustee-based structures – in order to develop expertise in all forms of social enterprise development and to continually develop models of support.

Social enterprise workers ideally would have experience of community development, enterprise development and a commitment to social enterprise. Their role would be to provide close project support on all aspects of project development, on a long-term basis. While project workers may need to undertake project management work, it is important that this role remains subservient to the overall governance and decision-making structures. The Social Economy Unit worked with projects in establishing 'enterprise management teams', which established a demarcation between operational functions and decision-making and policy functions. Social enterprise development should report always to the main governance structure of the project. An understanding of the community development context of social enterprise would be important in this context, because ultimately social enterprise is a mechanism for achieving community development aims.

---

37 For further discussion on support structures, see **Chapter 11**.

Alliances

A social enterprise support structure should develop alliances with public and private sector organisations as well as financial institutions (Lyon and Ramsden, 2006). Although community activists and organisations can play a key role in social enterprise development, Pearce (2003) is of the opinion that lack of expertise and resources within disadvantaged communities, arising from poverty, limits their capacity to develop social enterprises. Moreover, disadvantaged communities may lack the influence with State agencies around accessing support or assets with which to develop social enterprises. Alliances with entities from outside disadvantaged communities can help secure the necessary resources to develop social enterprises. However, this presents a key challenge for social enterprise development – while external expertise may be required, it is critically important that control of the social enterprise process rests with the community sector in which it is serving. Technical and external expertise can undermine group development processes – it is important that both are provided for, which necessitates a particular type of support, and one that can mediate relationships with external supports.

It is also essential that those with the technical expertise have some familiarity and understanding of these issues.

Case example: Waterford Social Economy Community Alliance and Waterford Crystal

Communities in Waterford city concerned with the high levels of unemployment and lack of services formed the Waterford Social Economy Community Alliance.[38] One of its key decisions was to develop social enterprises in disadvantaged communities in the city. Ultimately, it formed an alliance with Waterford Crystal to form the Waterford Local Economic Development Company, which developed social enterprises to alleviate poverty.[39]

---

38 The Waterford Social Enterprise Community Alliance was a network of social enterprises and community organisations committed to promoting social enterprise development in disadvantaged communities in Waterford City and with communities of interest such as Travellers.

39 The role of the private sector, including Waterford Crystal, in social enterprise development is discussed in **Chapter 10**.

THE ROLE OF A NATIONAL SUPPORT STRUCTURE

At present, the capacity of social enterprises in Ireland to contribute to the economic regeneration of disadvantaged communities is being constrained by the absence of a representative structure that lobbies on behalf of social enterprises. A national support structure would be required to fulfil this role, but also to fulfil other roles such as awareness-raising about social enterprise within the third sector as well as within the public and private sectors.

The national support structure also should consider the wider needs of social enterprises and propose models for their delivery. This includes such issues as access to finance, public procurement, alliance-building, and training. It should have a research and development focus.

Such a structure should be formed by social enterprises, as a national representative structure.

THE IMPLICATIONS FOR THE STATE

The State needs to acknowledge the need for social enterprises to receive specialist targeted expertise – provided by independent support organisations located in the third sector. The impact of these support structures would be only marginal unless the State is prepared to mobilise its mainstream enterprise supports for social enterprise development. For example, County and City Enterprise Boards (CEBs) should treat requests for supports from social enterprises no differently than those from private enterprises, and CEB staff should receive training in social enterprise methodologies. In acknowledging their role in supporting the development of enterprises, CEBs should engage with specialist support organisations in complementing supports provided and adding value to these supports.

Supportive state policy

A supportive State apparatus can mitigate immeasurably the many barriers experienced by marginalised communities attempting to regenerate their local economies. This will require the State, following meaningful consultation with the social enterprise sector, to develop a policy framework. It will require Government to direct local State agencies to support and resource social enterprises.

The State can play a crucial role through its policies and practices in creating the conditions for social enterprise to become vibrant. Central Government can enhance social enterprise development by:

- Formulating a long-term policy framework;

- Establishing an administrative unit within the Department of Jobs, Enterprise and Innovation to co-ordinate implementation of the policy framework;
- Assigning a senior civil servant to champion social enterprise development across Government departments;
- Establishing an innovation fund to assist social enterprises to grow;
- Directing State agencies to become more supportive towards social enterprises (Doyle, 2009).

State agencies

State agencies can enhance social enterprise development by:

- Broadening the perspectives of State agencies towards social enterprises, and recognising them as important stakeholders in the regeneration of disadvantaged communities;
- Training key personnel within State agencies and local authorities in social enterprise development;
- Ensuring statutory enterprise support structures afford the same range of supports to social enterprises as to private businesses;
- Supporting social enterprises to be in a position to tender for public contracts.[40]

CONCLUSIONS

Because of their mission, and a range of specific barriers that they encounter, social enterprises require a different type of support structure to private enterprises. Experience has shown that this targeted support is most effective when it is provided by third sector organisations. The communities that can benefit most are those in an area that has benefitted from community development activity for a considerable period of time. In the current economic climate, it will be challenging to develop sustainable support structures but the benefits to communities and the State would be significant, leading to employment creation, responsive services and providing economic self-determination to areas that have been economically disenfranchised by neo-liberal policies. However, the wider social economy sector, including the credit union and co-operative movements, could have a key role to play in supporting social enterprises through the provision of finance, purchasing

---

40 The potential for social considerations in the procurement process is discussed in detail in **Chapter 7**.

services from social enterprises, and providing expertise and training. This role would be consistent with the principles of co-operation.

5 Social enterprise in action – A Traveller organisation's experience

Anne Costello,
Margaret O'Riada
and Martin Ward

INTRODUCTION

Between 2006 and 2011, the Galway Traveller Movement (GTM)[41] initiated and developed a new model for Traveller social enterprise development, known as the Traveller Enterprise Development Unit (TEDU). It is a sustainable model that can be replicated by other communities of interest, and is an exciting and innovative step towards overcoming barriers to Traveller employment. TEDU has a key role in the development of social enterprises as a means of addressing Traveller unemployment and this chapter will provide an overview of the experience of GTM in developing the model.

THE GALWAY TRAVELLER MOVEMENT

GTM is a partnership of Travellers and settled people working together to achieve full equality for Travellers and the participation of Travellers in social, economic, political and cultural life as well as the broader enhancement of social justice and human rights. It was established in 1994 and works with Travellers in Galway City and South East Galway.

GTM is committed to the principles of community work: active participation, collective action, lobbying and campaigning at local, regional and national level to achieve positive social change for Travellers. GTM has developed strategic responses to Traveller needs in the areas of health, accommodation, education, justice and rights and Traveller economy and work.

THE CONTEXT AND RATIONALE FOR SOCIAL ENTERPRISE DEVELOPMENT

Travellers constitute a small indigenous minority ethnic group in Ireland with a shared history and a distinct cultural identity, customs and traditions that distinguish them from the majority population. The Taskforce on the Traveller Community (1995) suggested that visible markers of Traveller culture include "Traveller nomadism, the importance of the extended family, the Traveller language and the organisation of the Traveller economy …". Data from *Census 2011* indicates that there are 29,573 Travellers living in Ireland (CSO, 2012). However, according to the *All Ireland Traveller Health Study* (AITHS, 2010), there are 36,222 Travellers in Ireland, representing

[41] Further information on the process and activities of GTM and TEDU is available at info@gtmtrav.ie or www.gtmtrav.ie.

around 1% of the nation's population. Travellers' health, education, accommodation and employment status compares unfavourably with the rest of the population.

Traveller economy

The Task Force on the Traveller Community (1995) identified the importance of recognising the links between Traveller cultural identity and the traditional type of work that they undertake. It was of the view that a significant and distinct work-ethic exists within the Traveller community and that the Traveller culture and way of life values enterprise. The report provided an important insight into the unique nature of the Traveller economy explaining that "what distinguishes the Traveller economy is not so much the particular economic activities that Travellers engage in but the distinct manner in which these activities are organised". It recognised nomadism as a defining feature of many Travellers' lives. Other core elements include a preference for self-employment; an emphasis on income generation rather than wage labour; flexibility to quickly switch activities to avail of emerging opportunities; the involvement of the whole family (including extended family); and the home and work space are usually the same. According to the *Task Force Report,* those core features enable Travellers to make a profit in what are considered by others to be non-viable areas. The *Task Force Report* made 20 recommendations required to protect and support the Traveller economy and Travellers' participation in activities, including market trading, recycling and the horse trade.[42] It also recommended the exploration of the social economy as a support for developments within the Traveller economy.

Social enterprise

Social enterprise is recognised across the EU as a methodology and approach that can achieve success in tackling unemployment within marginalised communities. Marginalised groups, cultural minorities and ethnic groups have successfully established social enterprises to generate employment opportunities for long-term unemployed individuals, bring about social and economic benefits for geographical communities and communities of interest, and provide marginalised individuals with skills that are transferable to the mainstream labour market. Social enterprise can serve as a mechanism to overcoming barriers to employment and engaging in economic activity (Doyle, 2010).

---

42 In all of these three areas, subsequent regulation and legislation has undermined Travellers' involvement in these areas – for example, the *Control of Horses Act* and *End of Life of Vehicle Directive.*

GTM recognised that social enterprise can contribute to strengthening the practice of community development in many ways:

- Social enterprise can provide community development organisations with independent income over time, which strengthens their capacity to be more autonomous and sustainable and therefore to be in a stronger position to influence inequality in Irish society;
- It can provide a model of economic development which is concerned with promoting equality;
- It can enable Travellers (as well as other marginalised communities) to develop new skills that complement community development practice.

SOCIAL ENTERPRISE – ONE RESPONSE TO TRAVELLER UNEMPLOYMENT

Background

In 2002, GTM availed of an opportunity to become a partner in a one-year EQUAL[43] project led by Pavee Point aimed at addressing the exclusion experienced by Traveller men entrepreneurs. Fifteen Traveller men from Galway participated in the project. On completion of the project, there was a demand from the participants for continued support from GTM to develop their enterprise interests. As a result of this, GTM named work and the Traveller economy as a strategic area of importance in the GTM strategic plan 2004-2006. GTM recognised that it did not have adequate business skills internally and would need to contract in external enterprise expertise to assist the EQUAL participants, the GTM management, and staff to develop a vision and a strategy for Traveller enterprise development and employment in Galway. GTM envisaged setting up a structure that would support Travellers to engage in a range of enterprise development and employment activities: it was agreed that Traveller participation was a core requirement, for example, as directors, as managers and as employees. A decision was reached also to have a particular focus on recycling and the green economy. To date, two social enterprises have been established.

---

[43] The EQUAL Community Initiative was financed by the European Social Fund (ESF) and co-funded by the EU Member States within the 2000-2006 programming period. The initiative focused on supporting innovative transnational projects aimed at tackling discrimination and disadvantage in the labour market.

Recycling co-operative

At the time of development of the model, Travellers in Galway were recycling scrap copper wire in a manner that was dangerous to their own health and the environment. GTM engaged with other local development agencies in the RAPID Programme to seek to address the problems associated with this method of recycling in a manner that would not be detrimental to their health or their livelihoods. It was agreed to develop a project that would facilitate Travellers to continue recycling copper wire and other metals in a safe manner. Following extensive discussions and workshops with the men, a decision was made by seven of the men to form a workers' co-operative to run the copper recycling business – which was named Galway Recycling Co-op (GRC). Funding was secured for recycling equipment, as well as operational and training costs. An interest-free loan also was secured. While the co-op will not provide sustainable employment for all seven men, it will be of social and economic value to the community and also provides a blueprint for other recycling initiatives – in so doing, it will strengthen the Traveller economy.

Home insulation

TSA,[44] together with GTM and Traveller men, identified the potential in developing social enterprises that would create employment for Travellers and also meet unmet needs in the community. An opportunity was identified to seek funding from the Sustainable Energy Authority of Ireland (SEAI) to provide home insulation and energy advice to low income families at risk of fuel poverty, under the Warmer Homes Scheme.[45] Funding was sought from Pobal to employ staff under the Community Services Programme. Both applications were successful and GTM, trading as *First Class Insulation*, currently employs a manager and seven operatives (all members of the Traveller community) to insulate homes in Galway city and county.

Equality of opportunity for Traveller women and men

From the outset, GTM were committed to creating opportunities for both Traveller women and men within its enterprise development strategy. GTM is committed to creating further opportunities for Traveller women in social economy enterprises. GTM made a successful application to Pobal under the

---

44 TSA Consultancy, third sector advisors specialising in social enterprise development.

45 The Warmer Homes Scheme aims to improve the energy efficiency and warmth of homes owned by people on low incomes. It is operated by SEAI, Ireland's national energy agency, and is available nationwide.

Equality for Women Measure to support Traveller women to establish or expand their businesses.

A STRATEGIC APPROACH TO SOCIAL ENTERPRISE DEVELOPMENT

A number of barriers were encountered in establishing the social enterprises identified above. For example, GRC could not secure a lease on premises for two years, and all the evidence suggests that this was as a result of discrimination and racism directed at the Traveller community. Other barriers encountered included a lack of influence amongst State agencies, difficulties in accessing finance and access to business expertise.

Arising from these barriers, and following a number of exploratory workshops, it was agreed that a strategic approach to enterprise would be developed. The core features of such an approach were identified as:

- The development of a structure to support the development of enterprises and employment activities that would directly benefit Travellers in Galway city and county. This structure would be comprised of Travellers, representation from GTM, and enterprise/professional expertise:
    - The structure would endeavour to influence State agencies, Government departments, and other important stakeholders to provide funding, resources and supports to develop enterprises that directly benefit Travellers;
    - The structure would support the establishment of a combination of social enterprises (including worker co-operatives) and private enterprises owned by Travellers;
- The identification and implementation of measures to overcome barriers that stymie the development of social and private enterprises that benefit Travellers;
- The development of social enterprises to generate surplus income that could be used to benefit the Traveller community in Galway.

TEDU was formed in order to implement the strategy.

THE TRAVELLER ENTERPRISE DEVELOPMENT UNIT

TEDU was established and subsequently incorporated as an associate company of GTM, in order to oversee and drive the enterprise and work component of GTM. The establishment of TEDU was to become a key component of GTM's social enterprise strategy.

TEDU's mission statement is "to enable the Traveller economy in the Galway City area to grow and flourish, through assisting in the development of social and community enterprises, leading to economic benefits for the Traveller community in Galway". Its vision statement is that "by 2020, the Traveller economy in Galway City will be flourishing: where Travellers work in growing and innovative community businesses and private enterprises".

This structure is made up of Traveller entrepreneurs, staff and management from GTM and external expertise from the private business sector and the Galway-Mayo Institute of Technology.

TEDU is responsible for developing a number of social (as well as private enterprises) that will provide benefits to Travellers in Galway.

TEDU has the following six strategic objectives:

- Champion a culture that prizes and fosters community and social enterprise and helps these businesses to start and grow;
- Ensure that the support services provided (including access to finance) are accessible, relevant and of high quality to Travellers engaged in economic activity;
- Deliver or ensure access to high quality training opportunities so that Traveller men and women possess a range of skills either to secure employment or to develop formalised businesses;
- Provide sustainable employment to Travellers;
- Enable Travellers to generate an income;
- Create wealth for community benefit.

The model is underpinned by the principles of community development: for example, the participation of Travellers in TEDU is a fundamental feature, and resources are invested to ensure that Travellers are empowered to play a lead role in the development and implementation of the strategy and the model.

In developing the model to date, GTM and the social enterprises it has developed have received support and resources from the Department of Social Protection, RAPID and the Department of Education and Skills (under the 'Special Initiative for Travellers' fund).

CURRENT ACTIVITIES

GTM and TEDU focus on core areas of the Traveller economic development strategy. Some of TEDU's current activities and priorities are set out below.

Social enterprise development

TEDU will continue to develop social enterprises in order to generate sustainable employment, acquire new skills and gain qualifications for Travellers in Galway. The social enterprises will engage in activities that will have a positive impact on the environment. They will focus on recycling materials for which the facility to recycle does not already exist and which are either exported out of the country or go to landfill.

Alliance-building

Social enterprises can experience a number of barriers arising from poverty and inequality (Pearce, 2003). These can include a lack of expertise and lack of influence with State agencies around accessing supports. In the case of Travellers, racism and discrimination are additional barriers experienced. It is the view of GTM and TEDU that supports received from within and outside the Traveller community increase the likelihood of social enterprises achieving sustainability. Alliances have contributed to the development of TEDU and alliance-building will continue to be an important element in the strategy.

Contract work and procurement

Assistance will be given to social (as well as private) enterprises in tendering for contracts from State agencies and private enterprises. Contracts will be sought to retrofit local authority housing stock. In particular, TEDU will lobby for policies around social procurement as a mechanism for generating employment and training opportunities for Travellers.

Securing development capital

In the absence of a State social enterprise policy framework, and because of the difficulty for social enterprises in attracting grants, it can be very difficult for Travellers to diversify into new markets or to expand the existing business. This adversely affects their capacity to generate additional employment. Consequently, TEDU intends to develop relationships with philanthropic foundations, voluntary organisations and wealthy individuals to secure capital that will enable social enterprises to diversify and grow or to facilitate the formation of new social enterprises.

Business premises – Traveller-specific enterprise centre

GRC's difficulties in acquiring a premises over a two-year period demonstrates the difficulties for Traveller enterprises in finding industrial or commercial premises, and these are likely to recur. For this reason, the option of developing or purchasing a Traveller-specific enterprise centre is being examined, and TEDU is seeking funds to carry out a feasibility study on such an initiative.

Research

GTM intends to underpin its own work with on-going evidence-based research, action-based research and evaluation of its efficacy in accordance with best practice. GTM and TEDU will work with others interested in carrying out wider research on social enterprise models and opportunities as they exist, at a national and international level. This will support the case for a robust national policy framework and support structures for social enterprise and local social economic development.

For example, a recycling research hub will be established to identify, test and market products from waste materials. The products then will be sold, creating commercial opportunities for Traveller-led enterprises. This hub will be developed in association with a third level institution and other voluntary organisations in Galway city, and will draw from international best practice.

Communication and dissemination

Research highlights the pervasive discrimination and prejudice encountered by Travellers in Galway city and county (Irwin, 2006), fuelled by negative stereotypes of Travellers. In addition to campaigning for appropriate measures to be initiated by the State to tackle this discrimination, GTM intends to document and disseminate its work to showcase the high-quality service provided by *First Class Insulation* and other future enterprises, as a tool to challenge the negative stereotyping of Travellers. GTM also is sharing the learning from the TEDU model with other Traveller organisations.

Finally, it is within TEDU's remit to provide business support to Travellers (both male and female) who are committed to starting and/or expanding their own businesses. This will include the identification of barriers they encounter and strategies to overcome them.

CONCLUSIONS

GTM, with the assistance of State agencies, Government funding and voluntary organisations, has had a positive impact on the Traveller community in Galway through the provision to Travellers of employment, accredited training, and potential opportunities to generate income, through its social enterprise development work. The TEDU model has been a key component in the delivery of this work.

With continued support from State agencies, Government funding and support from philanthropic foundations, GTM will be in a position to break new ground regarding economic opportunities for Travellers living in Galway City. Indeed, GTM believes that the approach could be the blueprint for other Travellers' organisations to address the economic marginalisation that affects Travellers throughout Ireland.

6 Housing – an engine for social enterprise

Chris White

INTRODUCTION

Housing associations are not-for-profit companies that focus on the delivery of rented housing for vulnerable sectors of society. They represent a simple solution to a complex problem and have the capacity to be flexible, innovative and solution-orientated. Throughout Europe, housing associations and co-operatives not only are at the forefront of providing housing to social groups, but also are leading on a variety of related social issues beyond the built environment. Employment, education, training and mental health initiatives all have been led by voluntary housing bodies.

The voluntary housing movement in Ireland, whilst smaller than its counterparts in the UK and the US, still has an important role to play beyond its core function of housing provision.

The voluntary housing movement in Ireland is amongst the largest, best-funded and most active parts of the not-for-profit sector on the island. In 2009, the 400 housing associations in Ireland turned over in excess of €100 million.[46]

The voluntary housing sector in Ireland has grown rapidly in the last 15 years but has been in existence since the turn of the 1900s – this growth is similar to that experienced in philanthropic social housing development in Britain in the 1960s and early 1970s. The sector now has approximately 25,000 units of accommodation available to low income families, the homeless, the elderly and people with intellectual, mental and physical disabilities.

Housing associations are very much seen by the Department of the Environment, Community and Local Government (DoECLG) as the prime source of new housing units and potentially the acquirer of local authority housing stock in the future: "in recognition of both the constrained funding levels available for local authority construction programmes, as well as the capacity and track record of the voluntary and co-operative housing sector, approved housing bodies will be at the heart of the Government's vision for housing provision".

In the UK, voluntary housing associations have been significant drivers in the development of the social enterprise sector. The National Housing Federation (the representative body for all English and Welsh associations) undertook research that found that associations invest around half a billion pounds in neighbourhoods every year, two-thirds of which comes from their own resources. These investments focus on a range of social enterprise activity, including employment and enterprise, education and skills,

---

46 Source: research undertaken in 2011 by Boardmatch Ireland involving the reviewing of the annual returns of all 400 voluntary housing associations in the State.

wellbeing services, tackling poverty and financial exclusion, safety, cohesion, and environmentalism. The ability of housing association to make such interventions is dependent on their size. Housing associations in the UK are larger in terms of units in management, have a more established asset base and generally are very much seen in a corporate finance light (NHF, 2008). Irish housing associations are not yet in that position of overt financial strength, but the sector is moving in that direction.

In the UK, housing association growth has been supported by a number of policy measures from central and local government. This presents both opportunities and challenges for the voluntary housing sector. In this chapter, these policy measures are outlined, and possible considerations for Ireland are discussed.

BRITAIN

Policy context

'Housing plus' (Power and Richardson, 1996) has been a catch-all phrase used for a wide variety of activities by housing associations in England, Wales, Scotland and Northern Ireland. Becoming popular in the late 1990s and promoted by both the Housing Corporation[47] and various research bodies, it refers to all housing association programmes that are not core housing – thus housing development, maintenance or management are excluded, but all other activities are included. This might include such activities as a fuel poverty prevention programme, supporting the establishment of credit unions, and job initiatives or supported employment projects.

The housing plus attitude, however, has led to a surge of innovation around what broader impact housing associations can actually make on the communities and areas they work in and serve.

Some examples of UK housing associations that have social enterprise initiatives

The Eldonian Community-based Housing Association Ltd (Eldonians) was set up as a housing so-operative in 1983 by tenants from Eldon Street and Burlington Street in Liverpool. The homes of these residents were scheduled for demolition, which would have meant that the

---

[47] The Housing Corporation was the non-departmental public body that funded new affordable housing and regulated housing associations in England. It was established by the *Housing Act, 1964*. On 1 December 2008, its functions were transferred to two new organisations: the Homes and Communities Agency and the Tenant Services Authority.

community would have been broken up and the people relocated to different parts of Merseyside. The co-operative was set up in response to the proposed demolition. In 1990, the co-operative became a community-based housing association.

The Eldonians provide a range of services to the community in which they work as well as providing standard family housing: the services range from garden markets and garden nursery to accommodation for the elderly. The Eldonians also diversified into new markets, and act as management agents for 147 privately-owned apartments on three different sites. It provides services such as day-to-day maintenance, window-cleaning, gardening and the cleaning of communal areas on these sites.

Whaley Thorns and Langwith Village Company was set up by Leicester Housing Association. It has focused on regenerating former coal mine villages in the East Midlands and has taken on housing and economic regeneration. Incorporated as a friendly society, it operates a number of shops in the villages, a community resource centre as well as employment providers in terms of decorating companies, maintenance companies and landscaping.

TREES (Training, Regeneration, Education, Employment, Sustainability) Ltd is one of the largest social enterprise groups based in the Midlands. TREES promotes and supports social enterprise development through partnership working across the private, public and social enterprise sectors.

TREES originally was founded to create employment, training opportunities, local services and wealth in deprived communities across the Midlands. The TREES group includes several businesses that operate in a range of commercial and social sectors – from conferences, construction to cleaning and consulting. The project helped to launch Newlife Regeneration Construction in 1999. In 2002, the success of this company enabled the group to focus on developing Highpoint – a conference venue on the outskirts of Leicester city centre. TREES has also partnered with organisations (in the public, private and voluntary housing sector) and has developed the SPARK programme, a development and investment programme that aims to inspire organisations to build social enterprises that will prevent and tackle homelessness using sustainable business models.

However, a report commissioned by the Joseph Rowntree Foundation (Slatter, 2001) found that the term 'housing plus' as originally defined by

Power and Richardson (1996) was too narrow. It found that the practice of housing plus amongst housing associations had included a wider range of regeneration activities including training and job search schemes, retail development, money advice, family support, action partnerships with schools, youth work, art and sport projects, and community safety programmes (Power and Richardson, 1996).

LESSONS FOR IRELAND – EMERGING PRACTICE AND ISSUES

In comparison to the UK, the voluntary housing sector in Ireland is smaller, so it has not developed this model of social enterprise development. However, with the questionable success of standalone local government companies,[48] the model of public-private partnerships, there is an opportunity for large-scale regeneration project led by a housing association.

This opportunity is bolstered further by the fact that the model of housing associations will become the primary delivery mechanism for national government housing policy in Ireland. The DoECLG in Ireland has been very clear that it sees the future development of social housing as being the responsibility of housing associations (DoECLG, 2011): there is a financial imperative for this in that future capital funding is then off the national balance sheet. However, this is not without its challenges: public housing in Ireland is at a crossroads. Not only is there a shift in the primary provider of social housing (from local authority to housing association), but there is an increased expectation on what housing associations can deliver both locally and nationally.

AN ALTERNATIVE TO THE TRADITIONAL APPROACH TO REGENERATION

In Ireland, there is a poor tradition of well-maintained public housing. This can be attributed to the limitation of local and central government funding. Local authorities generate their income from a differential rent structure,[49] which limits the income they can generate from their housing stock. This, and

48 Of the Dublin Docklands Development Authority, Limerick Regeneration, North and South, and Ballymun Regeneration Ltd, only Ballymun was still active in mid-2012.

49 Local authority rents are based on a system called 'differential rents', which means that the rent is based on the tenants' ability to pay. If a tenant's income is low, their rent will be low; and if the tenant's income increases, so will their rent.

insufficient funds from central sources, means there has been inadequate funds to provide an appropriate planned maintenance programme.

The long-standing view of local authority housing departments has been to rely on central government-funded remedial works schemes for major refurbishment projects. With the restrictions on finance now very evident and stated Government policy of placing voluntary housing associations at the 'heart' of housing procurement and delivery, there is an opportunity for housing associations to look for transfer of local authority estates to them. Housing transfer from local authority to housing association, a long-standing policy in the UK, offers challenges to the sector but also significant opportunities.

The emphasis on physical regeneration has given way to regeneration and social enterprise, where additional tangible benefits can accrue to communities in the form of training, employment, community-owned enterprises, and communities having greater levels of economic self-determination.

Regenerating local authority housing estates is the best affordable social housing investment opportunity for the State at present, according to Clúid Housing Association, the largest housing association in the country. Clúid is (at the time of writing) the lead organisation on the regeneration of St Patricks, a local authority estate in Longford town.

VOLUNTARY HOUSING ASSOCIATIONS AND SOCIAL ENTERPRISE – OPPORTUNITIES AND THREATS

Housing associations in Ireland have the capacity to deliver solutions using a social enterprise model, and the housing policy context can assist them in undertaking these actions. The UK experience demonstrates that they can engage in social enterprise development in the following ways:

- Becoming more sustainable as organisations (building on their assets and expertise in property management and development). A market opportunity for supporting other voluntary housing providers could exist in Ireland;
- Contracting existing social enterprises in areas such as maintenance, as is the case in the UK;
- Establishing social enterprises in sectors such as care services to add value to their housing services and meeting current and future tenant needs.

However, this new opportunity is not without its challenges for housing associations in Ireland. As 'approved bodies', housing associations are regulated by DoECLG. The Department is wary of housing associations taking on additional risk-bearing activities, and is clear about this in its guidance on risk.[50] However, the application of this directive is very limited: housing associations in Ireland are very lightly regulated and have become accustomed to such an approach.

The proliferation of housing associations in the State is another cause for concern: the capacity for housing associations to impact on communities in a way similar to the UK is undermined by the small scale of the majority of associations in Ireland. The strategic review of capital funding schemes for voluntary and cooperative housing by Grant Thornton (2009) for the Centre for Housing Research highlights the fragmented nature of the sector, its over-reliance on capital funding from the State, and a lack of collaboration within the sector. The review goes on to recommend a specific initiative of housing association in Limerick (the Limerick Housing Services Company), which is a collaboration between housing associations in county Limerick, south Clare and north Kerry, providing housing management and maintenance services to the smaller housing associations in these areas. The report recommends that this model be used as a template for the sector.

CONCLUSIONS

While housing associations are social enterprises in their own right, they also can take a greater role in social enterprise development by initiating social enterprise activity as an element of regeneration. They have considerable access to resources; they can choose to support social enterprise by the awarding of contracts; and they can choose to support social enterprise by providing business accommodation, technical support, and provide a market for the goods and services produced by social enterprises. In doing so, they can contribute to a number of State objectives, including reducing long-term unemployment, up-skilling low skilled workers, and addressing fuel poverty, to name but a few.

---

50 "2.11 Organisations engaged in commercial or other risk taking activities should, in addition to (a) to (d) of Paragraph 2.9 also furnish information on the nature of the management structure and control procedures for the proposed housing project/s. To obtain approval under Section 6 of the 1992 Housing Act, such organisations would generally be required, where appropriate, to form a separate legal body complying in full with Paragraphs 2.3 to 2.10 with the sole purpose of operating the housing project/s. Approved housing bodies may not be controlled or be a subsidiary of another" (DoECLG, 2002).

For housing associations and local authorities to act as successful agents of change in the regeneration of communities and in the development of social enterprise, housing associations need to:

- Play a leadership role in identifying opportunities for social enterprise development and promote and develop appropriately targeted social enterprises in their area;
- Ensure that management boards or committees sign up to the principle of delivering or supporting social enterprise activities;
- Work together across Ireland to develop a practice exchange for housing associations, local authorities and other social enterprise organisations to share information on their activities that can encourage similar actions or projects in other areas;
- Ensure housing associations staff have the necessary knowledge and skill to initiate or support social enterprise activities;
- Engage with housing associations and community organisations locally to pursue appropriate social enterprise activities.

7 Procurement and social enterprise

Tanya Lalor

INTRODUCTION

The potential of public procurement[51] as a driver of economic development is hugely significant. Across Europe, public authorities' expenditure accounts for approximately 16% of GDP (European Commission, 2004). In Ireland, according to the National Procurement Service (NPS)[52] €15bn was spent on public procurement in 2010, with health (€4.6bn) and capital works (€6bn) accounting for over 70% of expenditure (Campbell, 2012).

Across Europe, social procurement (one of the terms indicating the use of social considerations in the public procurement process) has facilitated social enterprise development since the 1990s. For example, in the past, certain provisions in Italy favoured social co-operatives as well as bidders from less developed regions of the country. Dutch and Danish local government laws provided for requirements to create jobs among the long-term unemployed. German rules allowed favourable terms for bidders with a refugee background (Trybus, 2008). More recently, the issue has gained renewed momentum, with new policy initiatives being undertaken in such countries as Belgium and the UK.

In Ireland, the Social Enterprise Task Force (2010) has recommended the inclusion of 'social clauses' in the public procurement framework, as well as the development of a procurement support programme to assist social enterprises to build consortia and to tender for public sector contracts.

There is some confusion about how and when social considerations in the procurement process can be incorporated while complying with EU law.[53] The area is highly regulated, and some of the above examples have been challenged in the Court of Justice of the European Union (CJEU) by the European Commission (in particular, the Italian procurement laws).

The European Commission is currently revising public procurement law. In its *Green Paper* on modernising procurement policy, the European Commission (2011b: 5) states that "another complementary objective is to allow procurers to make better use of public procurement in support of common societal goals: these include protection of the environment ... and combating climate change, promoting innovation and social inclusion". It is anticipated that a new legislative framework for procurement will be in place in Europe before the end of 2012.

---

51 The acquisition of goods and services by the State, usually by means of a contractual arrangement after public competition.

52 The National Procurement Service (NPS) is located in the Office of Public Works and has been tasked with centralising public sector procurement arrangements for common goods and services.

53 For example, see Office of the Third Sector (2008).

In this chapter, the scope for public procurement to achieve wider social objectives and the implications for social enterprises, as well as for policy-makers, are considered.

SOCIAL PROCUREMENT – DEFINITIONS AND PRACTICE

The practice of using the procurement process to address non-economic issues is not new: for many years, selection criteria have been used to exclude certain parties who do not adhere to specified ethical standards. The US states of New York, Rhode Island and Massachusetts adopted policies requiring all contractors doing business with Northern Ireland to adhere to the 'MacBride Principles'.[54] And during the era of South African apartheid, public procurement policies that required adherence to the 'Sullivan Principles'[55] were common (Caron, 2003).

Currently, social procurement proposes the use of public procurement to achieve social objectives in a proactive way. In Europe, there are a range of terms used including 'socially responsible public procurement' (SRPP) (European Commission, 2010a), 'community benefits' and 'social issues' in procurement. These terms cover concepts such as compliance with social and labour rights; social inclusion; equal opportunities; accessibility design for all; targeted recruitment and training (TRT);[56] support for SMEs (including social enterprises) and minority enterprises (Macfarlane and Cook, 2008).

The term 'social clauses' is used also and has been defined by the UK's Cabinet Office (Office of the Third Sector, 2008: 5):

> Social clauses describe relevant, legitimate and value for money aspects of a procurement lifecycle which fulfil a particular social aim. This may include social requirements within the technical specification and award criteria or a contract, where they are relevant to the subject of the contract and compliant with public procurement legislation, as well as the UK's value for money policy (or equivalent commitment).

---

54 The MacBride Principles are designed to ensure that companies in Northern Ireland are non-sectarian, and provide a tool for evaluating the actions of a particular company.

55 The Sullivan Principles comprise two corporate codes of conduct, developed by the African-American preacher Rev. Leon Sullivan, promoting corporate social responsibility: the original principles were developed in 1977 to apply economic pressure on South Africa in protest of its system of apartheid; these were later expanded to increase the active participation of corporations in the advancement of human rights and social justice beyond the original South African context.

56 This term is used particularly in the UK.

The term 'sustainable procurement' also is used. This has been defined by the Sustainable Procurement Task Force (2006) as:

> A process whereby organisations meet their needs for goods, services, works and utilities in a way that achieves value for money on a whole-life basis in terms of generating benefits to society and the economy, whilst minimising damage to the environment.

Social contracting and procurement can be a contentious issue, depending on its context. Anthony Collins Solicitors and MacFarlane (2007) describe the contention thus:

> ... the procurement of training by a Government department (say from a college or private training provider) may be a 'social issue' but is not contentious because it is part of what they conventionally purchase. On the other hand, the purchase of the same training by a local authority as part of a works contract for housing renewal would be considered a 'community benefit' and could be contentious – both within and outside of the local authority.

A key feature, therefore, of social issues in procurement is the innovative way in which they are used to achieve social outcomes in a contracting context that conventionally may not have these requirements as defined outcomes (Anthony Collins Solicitors, 2006).

THE ARGUMENTS FOR SOCIAL CONTRACTING

There are two main arguments for social procurement. First, the 'value for money' argument points to the potential for government to lever social and community benefits in its procurement of goods and services. It argues that national and EU policies and objectives relating to sustainability can be advanced through social procurement.

Second, the 'level playing field' argument makes the point that organisations (such as social enterprises) that achieve social benefits in the delivery of services are disadvantaged in the procurement process. This is because of the additional costs associated with these social benefits (for example, provision of targeted training or employment). Such costs are not encountered by the private sector which is not driven by a social mission. As a result, the procurement process needs to take into account this social dimension to secure a level playing field.

THE LEGAL BASIS FOR PUBLIC PROCUREMENT – EU LAW

The legal basis for public procurement in the European Union is provided by the *Procurement Directives*,[57] which offer scope for taking account of social considerations in procurement, on condition that they do not undermine Treaty principles. These principles are:

- Non-discrimination on grounds of nationality or locality;
- Transparency of award procedures and related decisions;
- Equal treatment of those wishing to be awarded a contract;
- Proportionality;[58]
- Free movement of goods, services and workers.

These principles are key for the EU in achieving an internal market.[59] In essence, as long as these principles and the *Procurement Directives* are adhered to, social procurement is possible, and to this end the European Commission has published a guide to social procurement (2010a).

However, the introduction of social clauses in the procurement process needs to be treated with care, as there have been a number of cases concerning social issues in procurement involving the Court of Justice of the European Union (CJEU). These cases have influenced the *Procurement Directives* and establish important principles relating to the scope and limits of social procurement.

CASE LAW AND ITS IMPLICATIONS FOR SOCIAL PROCUREMENT

Social considerations and the subject matter of a contract

The relationship between the social benefit sought by a contracting authority and the goods or service that is being procured is critical, and has been the subject of much discussion and argument.

The *Concordia* (Finnish buses) case[60] is one of the most cited cases in relation to social procurement. This case concerned the award of contract for

---

57 Directives 2004/17/EC and 2004/18/EC.

58 That is, not to include contract terms or technical specifications that are far beyond that needed to deliver the contract.

59 The internal market of the European Union is a single market in which the free movement of goods, services, capital and persons is ensured and in which European citizens are free to live, work, study and do business.

60 Case reference: *Concordia Bus Finland Oy Ab (formerly Stagecoach Finland Oy Ab)* v *(1) Helsingin Kaupunki (2) HKL-Bussiliikenne* (2002) (C-513/99).

the supply of urban bus transport services. The procurement process included environmental award criteria (in this case, criteria relating to the level of nitrogen oxide emissions and the noise level of the buses). The inclusion of environmental considerations in the award criteria was challenged.

The CJEU ruled that contracting authorities were entitled to include environmental considerations in their award criteria, when assessing the most economically advantageous tender.[61] However, these criteria must adhere to the following conditions:

- Be linked to the subject matter of the contract;[62]
- Not confer an unrestricted freedom of choice on the authority;[63]
- Be expressly mentioned in the contract documents or tender notice; and
- Comply with all the fundamental principles of community law, in particular the principle of non-discrimination.

While the *Concordia* case was concerned with environmental criteria, it has been argued that the same principle applies to social criteria (ClientEarth, 2011a). And in May 2012, the CJEU decided that EU rules permit public bodies to evaluate tenders for public contracts using criteria "based on considerations of a social nature". In this case, the Court was examining the province of North Holland's use of fair trade criteria in award criteria for the supply and management of coffee machines.

This case was the first time that the court had the opportunity to consider a case where social (rather than environmental) factors were at stake in the award phase. In allowing award criteria to reflect social considerations, the Court ruled that such social criteria can have an impact on which tender wins the contract.

According to ClientEarth,[64] the ruling confirms that there are no grounds for treating social criteria differently to environmental criteria. The ruling will remove the legal uncertainty around the use of social criteria in public

---

61 Under procurement law, contracting authorities can award a contract to the cheapest tender or to the 'most economically advantageous tender' (MEAT) – this can include various criteria such as price, period for completion, running costs, technical merit, etc.

62 Attempts to include secondary or additional requirements that are not related to the subject of the contract can add costs and increase the risk of legal challenge.

63 In other words, there must be criteria in place governing awarding of contracts, and these must be specific and verifiable.

64 A not-for-profit legal organisation, comprising activist lawyers committed to securing a healthy planet.

procurement – something that ClientEarth believes has been holding back aspects of sustainable public procurement.[65]

The question arises as to how it can be established whether a particular set of social criteria is linked to the subject matter of the contract. This question relates to whether the social criteria are 'core' or 'secondary' requirements of the contract. Core requirements have been described as those that are "essential to the delivery of the contract" (MacFarlane and Cook, 2002).

In the *Concordia* case, the environmental criteria (emissions) were core to the procurement of buses, while in the North Holland case, the social criteria (fair trade) were core to the goods and services (supply and management of coffee machines) being procured, hence linked to the subject matter of the contract.

Contract performance clauses

While the *North Holland* ruling should widen opportunities for social procurement, the European Commission has already confirmed that social considerations can be facilitated (albeit to a more limited extent) in the form of 'contract performance conditions'.

The *Procurement Directives* provide that:

> … contracting authorities may lay down special conditions relating to the performance of a contract, provided that they are compatible with Community law and are indicated in the contract notice or in the specifications. The conditions governing the performance of a contract may, in particular, concern social or environmental considerations.[66]

However, contract performance clauses, or special conditions of contract, must not be part of the award criteria of a contract, and therefore cannot be used in the selection or the award process. This means that contracting bodies are not permitted to take into account whether economic operators or tenderers have the technical and professional capacity to deliver the conditions specified in the performance clauses until the contract is awarded.

In *Beentjes*,[67] the CJEU ruled that a contract performance condition (in this case, requiring the successful contractor to employ long-term unemployed persons) could be compatible with the procurement directives if it complied with Treaty principles, in particular the principle of non-discrimination, and was mentioned in the contract notice. The Court held that it could be

---

65 http://www.clientearth.org/blog/court-of-justice-gives-thumbs-up-to-social-aspects-in-sustainable-public-procurement, accessed July 2012.

66 Directive 2004/18 Art. 26; Directive 2004/17 Art. 38.

67 *Gebroeders Beentjes BV* v *The State (Netherlands)* C 31/87.

discriminatory if it became apparent that the condition could be satisfied only by tenderers from the Member State concerned, or if tenderers from other Member States could have difficulty in complying with it.

Local labour clauses are examples of provisions that could be discriminatory and contrary to Treaty principles, just as any other requirements for locality. It is generally held that they would be discriminatory, as they would disadvantage non-local bidders.[68] This has been ruled in other cases: in the *Insalud* case,[69] a requirement for a contractor to have premises in a particular geographic area was held to be discriminatory, and in *DuPont de Nemours Italiana and Laboratori Bruneau*,[70] it was found to be discriminatory to require bidders to obtain a set portion of their suppliers from a specified region.[71] The CJEU held that the Italian legislation discriminated against products originating in other Member States – and consequently, violated the Treaty principles.

However, clauses relating to the employment of those who are long-term unemployed, or disadvantaged in labour market terms, are permissible as these will not be directly or indirectly discriminatory.

One of the criticisms of contract performance conditions is that non-compliance can be addressed only retrospectively – for example, through breach of contract. ClientEarth (2011b) makes the point that "procurement procedures often can be very lengthy and costly ... public authorities may not be able to afford the time to start over the procurement procedure in order to award a new contract. And in some cases, it will be difficult to terminate a public contract during its performance". As a result, there may be little recourse for the contracting authority to challenge the non-performance of these clauses. For this reason, inclusion of social considerations at earlier stages in the procurement tendering process is preferable.

Enterprise ownership and procurement

It is important to note that ownership (of a company or organisation tendering for a contract) cannot be used as a basis for award criteria in the procurement process. The case *Commission v Italy*[72] found that it was

---

68 For example, see Anthony Collins Solicitors and MacFarlane (2010).

69 Case reference: *Contse SA* v *Insalud (now Ingesa)* (2005) (C-234/03)

70 Case reference: *DuPont de Nemours Italiana SpA* v *Unitá Sanitaria Locale No. 2 Di Carrara* [1991] 3 CMLR 25; *Laboratori Bruneau Srl* v *Unitá Sanitaria Locale RM/24 De Monterotondo* [1991] 1 CMLR 707.

71 Cited in Anthony Collins Solicitors and MacFarlane (2007).

72 Case reference: *EC Commission* v *Italy* [1991] 2 CMLR 115.

discriminatory to require contractors to be chosen from only companies in which all or a majority share of share capital was in public ownership.

SOME POLICY DRIVERS THAT CAN PROMOTE SOCIAL PROCUREMENT

Social procurement will take place only if there are policy drivers for organisations to do so. In the UK, a number of policy initiatives have been introduced that not only facilitate but require contracting authorities to pursue social outcomes from the procurement process.

Well-being powers

The 'well-being power' was introduced in England and Wales in 2000 (and in Scotland in 2003) to increase local authorities' capability to act on behalf of their areas. It allowed them to do anything they considered likely to promote the economic, social and environmental well-being of their area, unless explicitly prohibited elsewhere in legislation.

While well-being powers have been used by public authorities to good effect in some circumstances,[73] two recent legislative provisions in the UK may be more significant in embedding social procurement in public authorities' practice.

Social value duties and public sector equality duty

The UK's *Public Services (Social Value) Act, 2012* requires public authorities to consider how the services they are proposing to procure might add economic, social and environmental value, and how they will secure such changes in the procurement process. These obligations do not take precedence over the *Procurement Directives*.

Another legislative provision, within the *Equality Act, 2010,* requires public authorities to be more pro-active in ensuring equality of opportunity. This is known as the 'public sector equality duty', and is outlined in Part 1 of the *Equality Act,* which states that public bodies:

> … when making decisions of a strategic nature about how to exercise its functions, have due regard to the desirability of exercising them in a

---

73 For example, Nottingham City Council and Dundee City Council have gained commitments from some of their contractors (in construction and social care contracts) to provide targeted training and employment and have inserted community benefit clauses.

> way that is designed to reduce the inequalities of outcome which result from socio-economic disadvantage. (Section 1, Part X)

These measures are significant as they impose obligations rather than discretionary powers on public authorities. The public sector equality duty has been in force in the UK since 2011, but is underpinned by a range of policy measures in the UK – for example, the *National Procurement Strategy for Local Authorities*[74] in England and guidelines to public bodies for social procurement in Northern Ireland.[75]

THE PROCUREMENT CONTEXT IN IRELAND

In Ireland, public procurement has become the subject of attention across the wider enterprise sector, and it is viewed as having the potential to play a central role in Ireland's economic recovery. The emphasis has primarily been on improving access for SMEs.[76]

With regard to sustainable procurement, the Government's national green public procurement policy, *Green Tenders: An Action Plan on Green Public Procurement*,[77] asserts that:

> The scale of this procurement offers an additional and powerful policy instrument alongside more traditional instruments such as regulation, policy direction, and economic mechanisms like taxation, to 'move the market' in favour of the provision of more eco-efficient, less environmentally harmful goods and services. By taking into account environmental criteria in its procurement procedures, contracting authorities promote modes of production that are more environmentally friendly and stimulate greater supply of 'green' goods and services. (p.3)

Why is green public procurement firmly established in the policy arena, while social procurement is not? This is curious, as social considerations are

---

74 Department of Communities and Local Government (2008).

75 For example, Strategic Investment Board (2010).

76 For example, the Department of Finance (2010) issued Circular 10/10: *Facilitating SME participation in public procurement*, and in the current *Programme for Government*, the government asserts "We will reform public procurement to become a tool to support innovative Irish firms and to allow greater access to Irish small and medium sized businesses" (Government of Ireland, 2011: 10).

77 Department of Public Expenditure and Reform, and Department of Environment Community and Local Government (2012).

inherent in general definitions of sustainability procurement, including the one below cited in *Green Tenders*:

> Sustainable public procurement generally refers to the inclusion of environmental, economic and social criteria in the procurement of goods, services and works by public sector organisations.[78]

It is perhaps not surprising that a survey recently undertaken for the National Procurement Service[79] reported that, while 52% of procurers said that sustainability of the local economy is an important/highly important consideration for them, only 17% said that engaging with the not-for-profit sector is important or highly important. This compares to 60% of procurers stating that environmental sustainability is either important or highly important for them. The same research notes that "there is an opportunity for greater participation of social enterprises in delivering public services" (*Ibid.*, p.22).

It is worth noting that full procurement procedures only apply to goods and services over a certain threshold.[80] Moreover, the European Commission provides for a category of services (Part B services) that do not fall within the full procurement procedures. These include health services, education services and recreational, cultural and sporting services.[81] This offers significant scope for social procurement provisions for small social enterprises that would not be tendering for large public contracts, without the confines of full public procurement procedures.

CONCLUSIONS

In the current economic crisis, public procurement can help to secure social and economic outcomes, thereby adding value to ever-shrinking Government expenditure. The Government should consider developing a policy and action plan on social procurement (as has been in the case in other European countries), which could be implemented by the National

---

78 This definition of sustainable public procurement was used by Perera *et al.* (2007).

79 Procurement Research Group (2012).

80 The current thresholds are: €4,845,000 for the procurement of works; €125,000 for the procurement of supplies and so-called Part A services by central government bodies, and €193,000 for the procurement of supplies and Part A services by other public sector bodies. For goods and services below these thresholds, full procurement procedures do not apply.

81 Although there is no requirement for prior advertising or any form of competitive tendering to be carried out for Part B services, they still must adhere to general obligations such as transparency, equal treatment and non-discrimination.

Procurement Service. Confusion and concern around the scope of social procurement[82] underlines the importance of leadership in driving social procurement.

Actions in any strategy should include promotion, awareness-raising, and training in social procurement. Guidelines and templates on incorporating social considerations in public procurement also should be published for contracting authorities.

The introduction of a requirement for public sector organisations to have due regard to social benefits and equality in carrying out their functions (similar to the UK's public sector equality duty and the *Public Services (Social Value) Act 2012*) would have benefits far wider than social procurement – but it could also be a driver for achieving social benefits from the public procurement process.

The recent CJEU decision on the *North Holland* case could not be more timely, particularly as the European Commission prepares new procurement legislation. For Ireland, the *Action Plan for Jobs 2012* (DJEI, 2012) already identifies procurement as one of the issues to be considered in a report on the potential of social enterprise to be undertaken by Forfás on behalf of the Department of Jobs, Enterprise and Innovation. It is to be hoped that this may start the process of an engagement with social procurement in Ireland.

82 For example, MacFarlane and Cook (2008) and Office of the Third Sector (2008).

8 Finance and social enterprise

Kieron Brennan

INTRODUCTION

A study in 2003 on social finance in Ireland found that the majority of social enterprises believed that mainstream financial providers were not sufficiently meeting their financial needs (TSA, 2003). While this study is almost 10 years old, it seems that most of the issues raised in it are still relevant, with the added complication that funding is even harder to access today due to the difficult economic climate in which we find ourselves. At the same time, it is widely recognised that indigenous enterprises, including those in the social economy, can play a major role in regenerating the national economy, so it is vital that obstacles to obtaining finance for viable projects and activities are removed.

In this chapter, the status of finance for social enterprises and the barriers they face in raising finance are presented, as well as options and proposals for meeting future needs of the sector.

THE BARRIERS TO ACCESSING FINANCE

In the aforementioned study, financial institutions were seen as having "little understanding of the particular features of social economic activity, project development issues and of the funding conditions under which such enterprises operate" (TSA, 2003). This criticism remains valid in 2012. Conditions of funding such as personal loan guarantees from voluntary directors are not appropriate for social economy projects and constitute a major barrier to accessing loan finance for many of them. Mainstream banks are clearly more comfortable in dealing with the requirements of the conventional 'for profit' business sector (perhaps because this is the sector in which they themselves operate).

The lack of organisation within the sector for using its collective bargaining power in dealing with the banking sector was another issue discussed in the 2003 study. At that time, one mainstream bank in Dublin managed the assets and bank accounts of 52 community projects. These projects experienced difficulties in accessing banking support – for example, overdrafts – in spite of their collective contribution to banking business. In this respect, there was an interest in collective arrangements between projects – for example, through mutual guarantee schemes – as a means of achieving a stronger bargaining position with mainstream banks.

Some projects did have a good working relationship with their banks and stressed the importance of regular communications as a means of achieving this. However, the view was expressed that a lack of accountability of mainstream financial service providers with regard to measuring the social impacts or social contribution of their financial services means that financial institutions had no incentive to provide services to the social enterprise sector. This may have changed to some extent with the emphasis in recent years on corporate social responsibility (CSR), though often it can seem that 'for profit' enterprises simply are going through the motions in being seen to have CSR on their agenda.

One might expect that credit unions would have a closer affinity with, and understanding of, social enterprises and their needs and might be best placed to deal with them. However, lending to social enterprises comprises a tiny proportion of credit union lending, certainly less than 5%. This is not because credit unions are unwilling to lend to social enterprises; on the contrary, most would be happy to increase this percentage dramatically. However, it has never been a strategic priority for them, partially because of a lack of expertise in the assessment and management of 'business' loans. Their primary business and expertise is in personal loans and many do not have the skills or systems required to manage loans to commercial enterprises, including those operating with a social mandate. Most credit unions do not operate current accounts (a key requirement for businesses), though this will change in the short to medium term with the implementation of payment systems, which will give credit unions access to the clearing system.

Unlike many State-funded micro-finance providers, credit unions' first priority is the security of its members' deposits, and consideration for social enterprise development is secondary to that. This is particularly true in the current economic environment, with heightened concerns on the part of savers about the security of their funds. Where individual credit unions have engaged in social finance services and have supported community projects, usually it has occurred because an individual credit union member or director has championed and promoted individual initiatives or activities.

Credit unions operate within a 'common bond', usually a geographically-defined area from which they draw their membership. Normally, they cannot operate outside this area, one result of which is that they do not compete with one another. A more relevant result from a social finance perspective is that they can lend directly only to projects within their common bond, which may not be where the demand for funding is located. Therefore, we could have funding available in one area and a funding requirement in another and 'ne'er the twain shall meet'.

In addition, legal and regulatory obstacles can prevent a credit union from getting involved in social enterprise projects, particularly larger ones. For example, credit unions can lend no more than 30% of their total loans for periods in excess of five years. It is likely that most social enterprise borrowers would need to repay their loans over a longer period than this.

However, with some imagination, innovation and some legislative or regulatory changes, all of the aforementioned obstacles could be overcome and credit unions could become a key source of finance for social economy enterprises.

Of course, the mainstream financial service providers are not the only source of finance for the social enterprise sector. The Social Finance Foundation[83] (SFF) was established as a result of a 2006 Government initiative. The Foundation acts as a wholesale supplier of funding for social finance and is supported by the mainstream banking sector and has approved €28 million in lending to date. The SFF sources and distributes funding to specialist social lending organisations, which are then responsible for assessing applications and managing the lending process. For example, Clann Credo is the pre-eminent indigenous social lending organisation within Ireland and was established originally by the Presentation Sisters to enable religious orders to provide affordable loans to community, voluntary and charitable organisations, community businesses and social enterprises. Clann Credo also has done much to demonstrate that social lending is a worthwhile undertaking that can deliver benefits at a community level and the organisation has pioneered strategic developments at a national level in social finance.[84]

INNOVATIVE FINANCIAL TOOLS USED BY THE SECTOR

It is clear from the foregoing that a key factor in the difficulties experienced by social enterprises in obtaining finance from the mainstream providers is that the current range of financial products does not 'fit' the sector. Assessment systems, techniques and criteria are geared to conventional personal or business loans and are not appropriate for the different objectives and characteristics of social enterprise projects. In other words, their financial needs are being shoe-horned into a range of products that are unsuitable for their particular characteristics.

A number of credit unions have undertaken local initiatives for social and community benefit, usually by means of sponsorship and donations rather than the provision of loan funding. However, the *Final Report of the Commission on Credit Unions* (2012) took the view that there is a role for the

83 www.sff.ie.

84 www.clanncredo.ie.

credit union representative bodies in facilitating credit unions in getting more involved in social lending, particularly in the promotion of social inclusion. While this recommendation is mainly aimed at the provision of personal loans, it could be extended to include small, micro-finance-type loans.

One of the key recommendations in the report is that a formal process of engagement should be established between the credit union representative bodies and Government to determine safe ways to invest *collective* credit union funds into community projects, employment initiatives and co-operatives. The collective fund would be held and managed centrally, with appropriate expertise in social and community enterprise. This would be in addition to any loan funding that credit unions might provide and would deal with the problem of the common bond by allowing for the provision of funding where it is needed rather than the current situation where it can only be made available in the locality of the individual credit union.

These collective investments could be designed specifically for the social enterprise sector, with input from the sector itself as well as the credit union movement. It is arguable that, once such a scheme is established, there is no reason why similar schemes could not be set up in which other interested parties such as the mainstream banks and the National Asset Management Agency (NAMA) (or indeed private sector investors) could participate. Given the potential net return to the State, it should be possible to provide tax incentives to the private sector to encourage investment. If this wide level of participation could be achieved, social enterprise could play a huge part in the regeneration of the Irish economy. An alliance between the social enterprise and credit union sectors could lay the groundwork for the development of such a scheme.

Further impetus should be provided by the European Union's recent social entrepreneurship initiative, which has the objective of making it easier for social enterprises to obtain funding. The EU has committed to putting forward a European regulatory framework for ethical investment funds, to encouraging the development of micro-credit in Europe (specifically by improving the related legal and institutional framework) and to making social enterprises an investment priority of the European Regional Development Fund and European Social Fund. These commitments should help to remove some of the barriers mentioned above.

POLICY AND PRACTICAL MEASURES REQUIRED TO ADDRESS THESE BARRIERS

The biggest obstacle to credit unions providing funding on a collective basis as envisaged by the aforementioned *Final Report of the Commission on Credit Unions* (2012) is the Central Bank's *Guidance Note on Investments* (2006), which sets out the types of investment products in which credit unions can invest, together with the term limit (maximum duration of investment) and maximum amount that can be invested in each type. These limits were put in place to ensure that credit union investments are held in low-risk instruments, such as deposit accounts and government bonds. Investments in social enterprises do not fall under any of the permitted headings, so it would require a change of policy by the Central Bank to allow such socially desirable investments to proceed.

In addition, some flexibility on the part of the Central Bank would be required to enable the provision of 'business' loans to the social enterprise sector. The *Final Report of the Commission on Credit Unions* envisages a significant restructuring of the credit union sector, resulting in a smaller number of larger credit unions through a facilitated merger process. This should mean that the skills required for the assessment and management of business loans and relationships are more widely spread around the movement. Credit union representative bodies could provide additional central assistance to ensure that all of the required supports and systems are available.

Given that the report (involving as it did the Department of Finance and the Central Bank, as well as credit union representatives) is a consensus view on the future development of the movement, it seems that the mindset exists to tackle the necessary reform and changes. The next step is for the credit union representative bodies to put forward proposals for how a collective scheme can be operated in a way that keeps the associated risk to an acceptable level. In addition, the representative bodies will have to show how they can ensure that credit unions have the ability and support to provide loans to social enterprises on a prudent basis.

Finally, given the potential financial benefits to the State from social enterprise (for example, increased tax income from employees and reduced expenditure on social welfare), not to mention the potential social benefits, it seems reasonable to expect that the State would be prepared to contribute to the process in a tangible way. Tax incentives for private sector investors have been mentioned already and would be relatively simple to implement. It also seems eminently reasonable to expect that the State would be prepared to underwrite a portion of the risk involved in lending to the social enterprise sector. For example, the *Credit Guarantee Bill* provides for a State guarantee covering 75% of losses on qualifying loans to firms with growth and job potential. The inclusion of social enterprises in this scheme, or in a similar but separate scheme, would be of assistance. To avail of a guarantee under the *Bill*, the borrower is required to pay a premium to the State (2% of the loan balance, assessed and collected in advance) and there are a number of exclusions that might prohibit social enterprises from availing of the scheme. Perhaps a reduced premium cost and a more liberal exclusion regime might be appropriate for social enterprises.

CONCLUSIONS

It is clear that social enterprise can play a major role in revitalising the Irish economy but it is equally clear that the financial needs of social enterprises are not being met to the required standard by the mainstream providers. This is largely due to a lack of understanding of the unique characteristics of social enterprises, rather than any deliberate policy on behalf of the providers. Given their social ethos and remit, credit unions could and should play a much greater part in the provision of financial services to the social enterprise sector and the imminent restructuring of the credit union movement should facilitate this objective. This will require some changes to policy and legislation, but the will seems to exist to make these changes. In addition, some targeted assistance from the State, which will accrue huge benefits from successful social enterprises, would go a long way to improve the performance of the sector.

9 The private sector and social enterprise – a case study of Waterford

Senan Cooke
and Helen Kavanagh

INTRODUCTION

This chapter is being written at a time when the impact of the worst financial crisis in the history of the State is forcing policy-makers to review and evaluate the potential for economic growth across all sectors of the Irish economy. The collapse and retrenchment of the economy since 2008 in the wake of worldwide economic depression and the credit crunch has been as dramatic as its rise in the Celtic Tiger era. Current government strategies, the support and operating systems and structures around job creation are insufficient to deal with the challenges facing the country with the extraordinary economic circumstances that prevail.

Social enterprises and the private sector can engage with each other in many different ways. Social enterprises provide the private sector with an opportunity to enhance their business reputation through social responsibility programmes involving communities in which they are located.

The private sector can contract social enterprises for supply of services, and this type of engagement can be critical to sustainable outcomes for social enterprises. It can provide access to training and business know-how essential in building the capacity of people and communities. It can provide specialist expertise and input at board and operational levels. Flagship social enterprise projects, the more ambitious the better, often have greater appeal to the private sector as they are often more challenging and visible.

Private and social enterprise collaboration, if organised, can be broad-ranging and result in robust long-term partnerships of mutual benefit. This chapter explores how the private sector can play a greater role in the development of social enterprise. Case studies on two urban and rural social enterprises – Waterford Local Economic Development Company in Waterford city and DFBA Community Enterprises Ltd in the parish of Dunhill-Fenor in County Waterford – show how social enterprises have benefited from engagement with private enterprise.

THE POTENTIAL HAS YET TO BE TAPPED

Clark and Eustace (2009) put a conservative value on the total annual revenue generated by the sector in Ireland, excluding the credit union sub-sector,[85] to be in excess of €240 million, with an annual spend of over €230 million in the economy. They estimated that some 9,300 people were directly employed in

[85] With its network of over 500 local organisations, the credit union movement employed *circa* 3,000 people and had combined assets of €15.1 billion and savings of €11.9 billion in 2010 (SETF, 2010).

the sector, a further 5,100 jobs were supported indirectly and that, for each individual employed, at least one other person volunteers in the sector. The report also highlighted that a considerable proportion of expenditure of social entrepreneurs and enterprises is absorbed locally, both in terms of wages and for purchasing goods and services. Anecdotal evidence suggests that social enterprise is at least 50% more labour-intensive than the average private enterprise.

It is hoped that with the increased public and private sector focus and support, the scale of the Irish social enterprise sector will be aligned quickly with our European neighbours. The Social Enterprise Task Force (2010) sees the potential to grow the social economy sector (including social enterprises) from a current level of 3% of GDP to a target of 5% of GDP, generating 65,000 jobs and an output of approximately €13 billion over the next decade.

There is huge scope to expand this sector and to create thousands of additional jobs in that there are so many dormant resources available in communities and there is such a need to do so at local level to retain some form of viability and cohesion. There were never more people concerned about the future of their families and communities and more willing to participate in job creation measures if government developed more meaningful support programmes to enable new job creation projects to develop. Partnership between the sectors is key to realising this vision.

A STEP CHANGE IS REQUIRED

There is an urgent need for government to acknowledge the potential of social enterprise and to take steps to move it into centre stage with IDA and Enterprise Ireland as drivers of job creation. We have witnessed a subtle change in communities working with the private sector but it has a long way to go to realise the full potential of what can be achieved. Corporate social responsibility and philanthropy are relatively new concepts in Ireland. On the other hand, there is a long history of voluntary community service, infrastructure and commitment available that can prove a key ingredient in building viable social enterprises in the future. A step change is required by government and its support agencies in adapting to the needs of communities on unemployment and enforced emigration and how they approach its management. While other job creation options will continue to replace lost jobs, the social enterprise sector has yet to get its chance to prove how it can create new jobs that will be additional. It is a low cost job creation area, bringing additional benefits such as empowerment of the people, fostering of an entrepreneurial culture with intergenerational implications for self-reliance and sustainability,

Research undertaken by Prizeman and Crossan (2011) surveyed social enterprises and found that, while enterprises sourced expertise from the corporate sector, few considered the corporate sector to be important stakeholders. Almost three-quarters of respondents (74.7%) drew board members from the public sector, with 59.6% drawing members from the corporate sector. Corporate enterprises were deemed to be less important, with over one-quarter of respondents (26.6%) indicating that these kinds of stakeholders were 'not at all important' for their enterprise. These results indicate that there is a need for awareness-building within the social enterprise sector on the true potential for meaningful impact of private sector partnership and support.

WATERFORD LOCAL ECONOMIC DEVELOPMENT COMPANY AND WATERFORD CRYSTAL LTD

In 2001, representatives of the Ballybeg Community Development Project (CDP) approached Waterford Crystal Ltd to partner with them in developing social enterprise projects. The company, knowing the situation, had no hesitation in agreeing to get involved: Ballybeg had approximately 800 houses and a population of 4,000 people. It was one of the most disadvantaged communities in Waterford city, if not the most disadvantaged. A majority of Waterford Crystal employees, including management, came from the city and were well aware of the Ballybeg profile of disadvantage.

The Waterford Local Economic Development Company Ltd (LEDC) was quickly established and three social enterprise projects were selected. These were recreation, education and enterprise. The strategy was to add value to what already existed and to build cohesion, inclusion, improved qualifications and new job opportunities for the community that had an employment rate of 50%. There was a unique opportunity to develop a regenerative, integrated project that would match the needs of one side of the partnership with the resources of the other but the vision and will was missing. While a lot of good work had been done by the City Council and the Ballybeg Community Development Project over a long number of years to improve community infrastructure in the area, many endemic problems remained.

Waterford Crystal Ltd was the leading employer in the city and region from 1950 to 2009, at which time it went into receivership. The company funded an enterprise officer, a number of senior managers, the services of a project manager, lawyer, accountant and significant cash injections as required by LEDC. The board of LEDC included four representatives from Ballybeg and four from Waterford Crystal; later, it expanded to include representatives from Waterford City Council, Waterford Area Partnership and Waterford Institute of Technology. The broad representation was aimed at disseminating the learning from the pilot city-wide.

Up to 2009, the company had contributed over €500,000 in cash and in kind to Waterford LEDC. The company also exerted influence in leveraging a wide range of resources previously beyond the reach of the community. This engagement by Waterford Crystal with Ballybeg, where a number of its employees resided, helped to foster a progressive employee relations environment within the company.

Cill Barra Sports & Recreation Centre

The first joint venture project involved a state-of-the-art recreation centre to facilitate greater social and recreational interaction and to prepare the way for follow-on projects. The Cill Barra Sports and Recreation Centre became the first LEDC project. With 8,400 sq ft of floor space and costing €1.2m to construct, the project was funded in the main by government. The Cill Barra Centre project was delivered to specification, on time and under budget. The expertise of the project manager and his back-up resources available from the company was the key to this achievement.

Today, the Cill Barra centre has three full-time and one part-time staff, as well as approximately four people per year on work placements. Groups and organisations using the centre include various community groups, local schools both primary and secondary, local sporting organisations, Traveller groups, youth groups and projects.

The private-social enterprise partnership in Ballybeg faced many challenges over the years. These included:

- Building and maintaining a cohesive LEDC board;
- Balancing private sector drive for results with community democratic processes;
- A preponderance for discussion and analysis over decision-making and action;
- Excessive red tape and paperwork involved in accessing State funding;
- Reasoning that the State was to blame for the lack of facilities in the estate;
- The depth and intractability of socio-economic problems;
- Lack of action from State agencies on the removal of barriers and understanding of the benefits to be gained;

- Insufficient funds and resources;
- A legacy of poor personal relations between the State and community and an unwillingness of some State bodies to reengage in the process;
- Frustrations over the speed of progress.

DFBA COMMUNITY ENTERPRISES LTD AND WATERFORD CRYSTAL LTD

In 1993, inspired by a strong GAA ethos of commitment to people and place, DFBA Community Enterprises Ltd (DFBA) was formed. DFBA is a financially-sustainable (self-financing as distinct from grant-aided) social enterprise established in the parish of Dunhill-Fenor in County Waterford. DFBA (the 'DF' represents Dunhill-Fenor and the 'BA' represents Boatstrand and Annestown, two other areas of significance in the parish) is a self-financing company limited by guarantee with charitable status. Its mission is "to develop the community socially, economically and culturally using the resources available".

In 1999, Dunhill Rural Enterprises Ltd (DREL) was established as the enterprise arm of DFBA. The company is limited by guarantee with charitable status. It has a voluntary board of directors with a wide range of business expertise. DREL issued a loan prospectus which was supported by 110 people and realised over €100,000. This helped to get the company up and running. A key operating principle is that every effort is made to source expertise, materials, equipment and cash free from the private sector. It is also a principle that, when purchasing supplies, DREL shops locally, regionally and nationally in order of preference, provided cost, quality and service are up to standard.

Since the foundation of DFBA, Waterford Crystal Ltd, together with other local businesses, has contributed specific expertise, funds, materials and equipment. It also has supported DFBA developments publicly, providing DFBA with additional influence in dealing with suppliers, agencies, politicians, business and civic leaders. The benefits of private sector involvement in DFBA activities includes:

- Increasing resources and capacity to achieve what could not have been contemplated beforehand;
- Boosting the confidence and capacity of volunteers and community;
- Changing perceptions of others of the vision and the capacity to realise it;
- Affirming the worth of projects that can open so many other doors;
- Providing valuable practical support when required;

- Getting things done: it is easy to establish a good fit between committed volunteers and private sector as the energy, drive, commitment and innovation is there on both sides;
- Significantly improving public relations and promotional opportunities;
- Improving the capacity to attract new volunteers and new resources of all kinds.

CONCLUSIONS – GAINING THE BEST FROM BOTH WORLDS

There is much more scope for building synergy between social and private enterprise on job creation and income generation over the next decade. Many local social entrepreneurs are motivated to tackle social need and deprivation or to avail of an outstanding business opportunity with a social focus. Social deprivation is often a sensitive area that creates a lot of argument with agencies on root cause and best solutions. Corporate sector involvement invariably brings objectivity, commercial nous and instinct to the table. The corporate sector also brings powerful networks of influence and expertise.

The philosophy and structure of social enterprise engages ordinary people in local enterprise projects. Social enterprise offers challenging work and training opportunities that address workforce and unemployment needs in a recovering economy.

The challenges involved for the private sector include:

- Ensuring project ownership is retained by the community;
- Avoiding the possibility of a dependency culture evolving;
- Developing a professional relationship with clear objectives and timelines;
- Building a skill base for community/project leaders to ensure sustainability;
- Developing a support network to ensure viability;
- Stepping back while maintaining a watching brief to ensure future progress.

Private enterprise is somewhat removed from the hardship inflicted on communities by bad planning and design at central and local government levels. Partnerships and joint ventures between private and social enterprises will promote greater understanding of the most practical and cost-effective solutions. Partnerships are likely to produce a level of innovation that can make all the difference to project managers and volunteers. Private enterprise will bring with it business expertise, financial, legal, marketing, logistics, human resources, quality, systems, decision-making, problem-solving and project management skills and experiences to the community project. It also will bring influence, network contacts, purchasing power, finance and, most of all, a degree of confidence that will enable that which could not be considered without these resources.

There is no best way of approaching the private sector for support. Needs and opportunities present themselves and the what, why, how, when and where follow on quickly – in particular, if the social enterprise promoter is aware of the benefits to be gained.

The Dunhill and Ballybeg experiences in working with the private sector on social enterprise projects have been very positive. Where social enterprise projects help to reduce unemployment and emigration, private industry is even more likely to engage with the community. There is a need for further and extensive research on how corporate Ireland can engage with local community-based social enterprises on job creation at this time of national crisis. If its potential is recognised and taken seriously, thousands of additional new job opportunities and hundreds of new enterprises can be created countrywide over the coming decade. It is a worthy objective for government to pursue this target with every resource at its disposal today. Social enterprise collaboration with the private sector is an under-rated and under-employed resource and its time has now come.

10 Social enterprise in Sweden and Scotland: local and national responses

Tor Justad

INTRODUCTION

The social economy in the EU employs over 11 million people and constitutes 6% of total employment.[86] At the *Promoting Social Entrepreneurship* in Europe conference on 18 November 2011 in Brussels, which has been lauded as the EU's most significant intervention on social enterprise to date, Commissioner Barnier stated that the European Commission:

> ... wants to facilitate social enterprise's financing, not just with European money, but also through other funding, including a social investment fund. We want to raise awareness about these businesses, promote networking, labels and certification. We also want to create a more favourable legal environment, for instance by enabling easier access to public procurement for social enterprises.

Among the proposed measures that will contribute to these objectives are reform of public procurement, a new investment priority, and financial support (over the period 2014 to 2020) through the Programme for Social Change and Innovation. Under this programme, nearly €100 million will be allocated specifically to promoting social experimentation, and another €90 million to supporting social enterprises.

Whilst these proposals have been welcomed, the policy and practice of supporting social enterprises varies considerably between EU Member States. In some countries, there is specific legislation that benefits social enterprises whilst, in others, there are a variety of funding regimes and support structures.

One example of this is the Italian *Law 381*, introduced in 1991, which recognised social co-operatives on the basis that the primary beneficiary is the community, or groups of disadvantaged people. For the first time, the law provided that these groups no longer have to be members of the co-operative, and so the concept of beneficial ownership was provided for in law, whereby social co-operatives were required to fulfil their activities "for the general benefit of the community and for the social integration of citizens". The law also provides tax benefits to social co-operatives.

Another example is Finland, where – from 1996 – new co-operatives for the unemployed have been eligible for self-initiative support from the Ministry of Labour covering 80% of start-up costs.

This chapter will examine practices in Sweden and Scotland that support the sector.

---

86 www.ec.europa.eu/enterprise/policies/sme/promoting-entrepreneurship/social-economy/.

SWEDEN

Key policy drivers for social enterprise and their political context

Sweden has a long tradition of an active civil society, institutionalised in the *folkrörelse* (people's movement) and in the co-operative movement. The *folkrörelse* is characterised by a large number of associations; historic links to the worker, temperance and religious movements; an emphasis on democratic governance; and a large membership base and active membership.

At national level politically, there is support for social enterprise across the political spectrum and a growing level of recognition of social enterprise from mainstream business, government, as well as wider society as evidenced by the inclusion of social enterprise in the manifestos of all the main political parties. There is recognition by business and government that social enterprise has an important role to play in creating employment and providing services, particularly related to vulnerable people in society.

Social enterprise in Sweden is regularly associated with the delivery of services such as childcare, education and health services. Much of this activity emerged as a response to cycles of privatisation in these sectors, an activity that was ended by social democratic governments which prohibited profit-making companies delivering private care. And so, social enterprises developed as a vehicle for service delivery.

However, the main policy driver now for social enterprise development is labour-market oriented – and social enterprise is increasingly reduced to being solely a labour market policy measure. Stryjan (2004) notes that, within the Swedish welfare state, the right to employment in Sweden is perceived as a general civic right, and work integration has been a public responsibility since the 1930s.

Defourny and Nyssens (2008) support this assertion, noting that "the term social co-operative (*sociala kooperativ*) has become synonymous with *work integration social enterprise*". However, Defourny and Nyssens also acknowledge the role of the social enterprise sector in the delivery of personal services, and Fraisse *et al.* (2007) note that childcare is a major field of activity of social enterprises in Sweden (as well as France), arising as a response to public provision shortage.

Key elements of support structures

The State is a key funder of supports for social enterprises, and takes on the role often played by philanthropic and other funders in other Member States.

However, the well-established co-operative movement in Sweden has meant that there is a pre-existing infrastructure for delivering supports for social enterprises, and the majority of social enterprise supports are delivered by the sector itself.

State agencies such as *Tillväxtverket* (Swedish Agency for Economic and Regional Growth) support a national organisation known as Coompanion Sweden,[87] which is a key support structure for social enterprises. Coompanion comprises 25 co-operative development agencies (CDAs), covering all 21 counties in Sweden and employing approximately 125 professional advisors.

This has meant that a support service is available in every part of Sweden – urban and rural – with wide-ranging support, including business, legal and funding advice. Being located within the social economy sector also enables Coompanion (n.d.) to adopt what it describes as a "method of work the co-operative advisers use [which] is outreaching, mobilising, problem-solving, process-oriented and educational". This method acknowledges the need for close project support over a long period of time, stating that "the co-operative advisers often have to act as supervisors during long mobilisation and development processes".

As it is located within the co-operative and social economy sector, Coompanion itself acts as a driver for new initiatives, and often initiates regional partnerships and programmes. The constituent CDAs in Coompanion also have formed a Swedish Association of Co-operative Development Agencies, which strengthens the sector through lobbying and representation, benefiting social enterprises as well as the wider co-operative sector.

Whilst Coompanion traditionally supported new co-operatives (typically running childcare and eldercare), in recent years its emphasis has been more on supporting social enterprises involved in engaging with vulnerable groups and the integration of vulnerable people into the labour market through setting up social firms.

The social economy sector in Sweden has maintained links with various parts of the 'people's movement' and has managed to negotiate continued support, although some levels of funding have reduced in recent years and more specific targets have been introduced related to specific work with long-term unemployed. So whilst the sector has developed its own support methods, these have resulted in some cases from changes introduced by the State related to conditions attached to funding.

Since the mid-1980s, Coompanion has received financial support from the State: at present, Coompanion is two thirds-financed on a regional basis by organisations, the public sector, consultancy income and EU funding. The

87 www.coompanion.se.

Swedish Government, through *Tillväxtverket*, provides the remaining one-third of its funding. The financing enables it to offer some of its advisory services free of charge.

Other forms of support for social enterprises – for example, social procurement and provision of social clauses in the procurement process – is undeveloped in Sweden, in comparison with other EU countries, according to Defourny and Nyssens (2008). They make the point that Swedish interpretation of EU public procurement legislation has not provided for the inclusion of social considerations in the procurement process.

Key success factors

Key success factors and defining characteristics must be seen in the context of a welfare State system and social democratic governments almost continuously since the 1940s. The key outcomes from the Swedish experience have been a vibrant childcare sector within the social economy – run by parents and staff. In Sweden, childcare services are clearly a major field of activity for social enterprises, which are often set up and managed by parents and professionals as a response to a public provision shortage (Fraisse *et al.*, 2007). Moreover, there are examples of co-operatively run schools – run by parents, and workers.

The existence of a national support structure providing advice and support, which is itself part of the social economy, has been an important feature. This is underpinned in the Swedish example by a vibrant co-operative movement that shares many values and principles of social enterprises and leads to a wider public understanding and support for social enterprises.

Finally, broad political consensus on the role and value of social enterprises, based on the important role of the 'people's movement' in the development of local initiatives, is a key feature.

The lessons for Ireland

The Swedish experience points to the important role of civil society in supporting the social economy, as it builds on work done by other parts of the 'people's movement' such as large organisations involved in informal adult education and the State church involved in social economy initiatives. Moreover, long-term national support structures, which themselves are based in the social economy sector, enables them to take a strong advocacy and developmental role at regional and national level. However, this is facilitated by financial support from the public and business sectors, and in addition to

State support, cross-party political support for social enterprises should ensure the continued development of the sector.

SCOTLAND

In Scotland, the co-operative movement can trace its roots back to the Fenwick Weavers' Society[88] which, in 1769, commenced retailing food. The consumer co-operative movement is still strong in both urban and rural parts of Scotland. While the term 'social economy' is not as commonly used in Scotland as in Ireland, the term 'social enterprise' has been widely adopted.

The Social Enterprise Network Scotland (SENSCOT) has promoted five criteria applicable to social enterprises, namely that they:

- Have social and /or environmental objectives;
- Are trading businesses aspiring to financial independence;
- Have an 'asset lock' on both trading surplus and residual assets;
- Cannot be the subsidiary of a public sector body; and
- Are driven by values – both in their mission and business practices.

At March 2009, turnover of the social economy sector as a whole in Scotland stood at £3bn – an increase of 4.3% on the previous year.[89]

Key policy drivers for social enterprise and the political contexts

The key policy drivers in Scotland for social enterprise development in the 1980s and 1990s were related to levels of unemployment and in integration of vulnerable groups into employment in social enterprises or 'community businesses' as they were commonly known at that time. In more recent years, the focus has moved towards the opportunities for the social economy in public sector procurement through contracting and an emphasis on growing the social economy and increasing the longer term viability of social enterprises.

As part of the UK, Scotland has strong links with the social enterprise sectors in England, Wales and Northern Ireland. Notwithstanding this, policy developments in England and Wales in the early 2000s (such as the establishment of the Social Enterprise Unit (SEnU) in the Department of Trade and Industry, and subsequently the Office of the Third Sector) were independent of Scotland, as social enterprise is a devolved function and included in the remit of the Scottish Parliament (established in 1999). In fact,

---

88 www.thefenwickweavers.com.

89 http://www.scotland.gov.uk/Topics/Statistics/Browse/Business/TrendSocialEconomy.

the view of social enterprise agencies such as the Scottish Social Enterprise Coalition (now Social Enterprise Scotland) was that – in its initial years – devolution had served social enterprises poorly, and that positive policy initiatives in England and Wales compared favourably to what the Scottish Executive was undertaking (Hutton, 2005).

However, since this time, the Scottish Government has taken a more pro-active lead in policy terms.

In 2006, the Scottish Parliament instructed the preparation of a 'differentiated strategy for social enterprise'. Published in 2007 (Scottish Government, 2007), this was regarded by SENSCOT (2009) as "an impressive document [which] set out an infrastructure which could have given the Scottish social enterprise community an international reputation". However, SENSCOT did not view favourably the subsequent policy perspective of the Scottish government that included social enterprise as part of the generic third sector: it noted that "we believe that this lowering of focus and profile is a mistake – a failure to grasp what's happening on the ground. Regardless of government, many of us believe that social enterprise, as a movement, continues to develop a distinct identity which adds value to developments in the public, private and third sectors. We believe that the promotion of its particular qualities should be increased not diminished and that our movement is accelerating" (SENSCOT, 2009).

The current Scottish National Party Government (from May 2011 with an overall majority for the first time) also has declared its support for the sector. At this point, it can be argued that devolution of many powers to the Scottish Parliament generally has had a positive impact in the development of Scottish institutions and social movements. One example of this is the establishment of Social Enterprise Scotland, which has brought together social enterprise intermediaries.

The Scottish Government places social enterprise within the context of the overall third sector, and reiterates its commitment to the development of an enterprising third sector in Scotland. Over the next three years (2012-13 to 2014-15), the Scottish Government is committed to providing a further £73.5 million to the third sector as a whole.[90]

Some UK-wide policies related to the social economy in Scotland

Obviously, there are some UK-wide programmes that impact as much in Scotland as in other parts of the UK. For example, the Department of Work and Pensions (DWP) 'Work Programme', introduced in 2011, is a supported employment programme and social enterprises can access employees under

---

90 http://www.scotland.gov.uk/Topics/People/15300.

the programme. The Work Programme is described by the DWP as providing tailored support for claimants who need more help to undertake active and effective job-seeking.[91] However, the programme has been criticised by parts of the social enterprise sector as it is viewed as having a potentially negative effect on opportunities for employing vulnerable and long-term unemployed people.

Support infrastructure in Scotland

Support structures in Scotland have developed and changed since the 1970s, and a variety of agencies and policies have been initiated in the intervening period. Current support structures include agencies operating at UK, Scottish and regional (Council) levels.

In the UK as a whole, the co-operative enterprise hub is a one-stop shop for free advice, training and access to finance for new and existing co-operatives.

The support infrastructure in Scotland is well-developed and has the capacity to cater for different types of social enterprise, in different regions of the country. The sustainability of the support infrastructure is facilitated by the commitment of the Scottish government towards social enterprise development. The support structure includes national and regional organisations, as well as consortium approaches to the delivery of social enterprise support.

National supports

Support for social enterprise in Scotland is characterised by a number of intermediary organisations, which support, lobby and advocate for the sector, as well as providing direct support to social enterprises. The Scottish Government provides support to the social enterprise sector in different ways, including the funding of these intermediary bodies. At national (Scottish) level, these bodies include:

- Social Enterprise Scotland[92] (SES), which is also the national promotion and lobbying organisation for social enterprise in Scotland;
- Social Firms Scotland (SFS), a national support body for the development and promotion of social firms in Scotland; and
- Social Enterprise Network Scotland (SENSCOT).

Amongst its activities, SENSCOT supports local social enterprise networks (LSENs), which are groups of active social enterprises that come together

91 http://www.dwp.gov.uk/policy/welfare-reform/the-work-programme/.

92 Formerly the Scottish Social Enterprise Coalition.

regularly in an effort to grow opportunities for themselves and their sector locally.

The Scottish government also provides support to Co-operative Development Scotland (CDS), which is a subsidiary of Scottish Enterprise – a Scottish Government economic development agency.

Specialist training support is provided by the Social Enterprise Academy, which was set up in 2004 as a social enterprise. It provides learning and development for those working in social enterprises.

Regional support structures

The support structure for social enterprises includes regional rural support structures as well as supports for specific sectors – for example:

- Community Enterprise in Strathclyde (CEiS) provides support on a regional basis;
- Firstport supports new and emerging social entrepreneurs across Scotland;
- Highlands and Islands Social Enterprise Zone (HISEZ) operates in the highlands;
- Rural Environmental Action Project (REAP) is based in the North East of Scotland, and supports social enterprises there as well as environmental initiatives; and
- Argyll and Bute Social Enterprise Network (ABSEN).

For specific sectors, there are also organisations such as the Scottish Agricultural Organisations Society (SAOS), which supports agricultural co-operatives, and the Community Retailing Network (CRN), which supports community retailing.

Collaboration between support organisations

The social enterprise sector in Scotland is on a scale that allows different support agencies to co-operate and share ideas and programmes. As a result, there are some key alliances – for example, Social Enterprise Scotland works closely with SENSCOT and SFS in lobbying the Scottish Government and other bodies.

An example of collaboration across the sector is the establishment of Just Enterprise (JE), a consortium of Scotland's key social enterprise support agencies to provide business support and development services to third sector organisations across Scotland. Its main role is to deliver the Scottish Government's contract for Business Support to the enterprising third sector.

The key elements that all these support structures have in common is providing business support, training, networking, signposting to funding streams or lobbying, and promoting the social enterprise sector.

Financial supports

One of the loan funding streams for social enterprises is Social Investment Scotland (SIS), a registered charity and social enterprise that provides business loans to third sector organisations.

Other funding supports included the Enterprise Growth fund for third sector organisations (now closed), which comprised a £6m grant fund, and the Social Entrepreneurs Fund, which was aimed at individuals who want to set up and run a business with a social or environmental purpose, and provided start-up funding (until March 2012).

The UK-wide Big Society Capital Fund was launched in April 2012 for investment in the 'social sector'.

Public procurement supports

Supports for public procurement and social enterprise have been central to government policy in the UK around social enterprise development. The Scottish Government also supports initiatives around public procurement, and the Developing Markets programme for the period 2011-2014 includes a number of measures to support third sector engagement in public procurement, including the development of community benefit clauses. This complements other initiatives and activities including the Procurement Reform programme and the *Sustainable Procurement Action Plan*.

Recent and emerging initiatives

A number of recent UK-wide initiatives may have an impact on social enterprise in Scotland over the forthcoming years. These include the *Social Value Act, 2012*, which requires public authorities to have regard to economic, social and environmental well-being in connection with public services contracts and requires local authorities to consider how the services they procure might add social, environmental and economic value.

Another mechanism gaining momentum in the UK, but which is yet to take hold in Scotland, is 'social impact bonds' (SIBs).[93] These provide up-front funding for prevention and early intervention services, and remove the risk that interventions do not deliver outcomes – the public sector pays if (and

93 A social impact bond is an outcomes-based contract in which the public sector undertakes to pay the service delivery organisation for significant improvement in social outcomes for a particular target group.

only if) the intervention is successful. The resulting financial products are described as forging links between the market, government and society for the greater good.[94] However, SIBs generally have been received negatively in Scotland and only a few examples have been implemented (including in 2012, Perth and District YMCA, which has attracted investment in its work with young people).

Finally, a cross-party Social Enterprise Group in the Scottish Parliament was established in 2011 – it has met on three occasions thus far, and so its full value is still to be judged.

Key success factors

Perhaps the most significant factor in the development of support structures for social enterprises in Scotland has been the ability of the sector to organise itself and lobby for support. The well-developed support structure meant that there was expertise within the sector on funding streams – including at EU, UK and national levels – as well as committed social enterprise managers and boards with considerable expertise (developed since the 1970s). However, the experience also demonstrated the importance of having a willingness to be flexible in response to changing political and funding realities.

The key outcomes for Scotland include a mature social enterprise sector developed from dynamic, innovative and committed individuals and organisations.

Key for Ireland

Lessons for Ireland from the Scottish experience of social enterprise development include:

- The need for a variety of specialist support structures tailored to different activities (business advice, training and funding), models (co-operatives, social firms, credit unions, housing associations etc.) and activities (retailing, agricultural, recycling, etc.);
- The value of a national promotional and lobbying organisation;
- The need for support and training (through the Social Enterprise Academy) in both urban and rural areas;
- The need to engage with relevant government departments and officials to argue the case for social enterprises to be supported as part of a national economic strategy.

---

94 www.socialfinance.org.uk/Vision.

CONCLUSIONS

The Swedish and Scottish examples indicate the importance of structures at national and local level, and their respective specialist functions: lobbying, networking, and awareness-raising activities at national level; and direct support at local level. The location of most of the support structures within the social enterprise or co-operative sector itself is important in ensuring that supports can adequately meet the needs of the sector, and are underpinned by an understanding of what social enterprises are trying to achieve.

Likewise, the role of the State is important in facilitating social enterprise development. However, it is important that the sector is not hamstrung by a government policy that emphasises labour market integration as the sole function of social enterprises.

11 The European Union as a champion for social enterprise

Erdmuthe Klaer-Morselli

INTRODUCTION

This chapter will provide an insight into several recent EU initiatives influencing social enterprise – the discussion and use of the term 'social enterprise' follows the perspective of social enterprises that emerge out of social economy.

Social enterprises emerging from the social economy do not only have a social mission. They also have specific values and a method of doing business – for example, co-operation and participation of members, employees and even clients in developing strategies of an enterprise.

SOCIAL ECONOMY/SOCIAL ENTERPRISE AND THE EU – SETTING THE FRAMEWORK

EU legislation has a significant impact on the social economy as a whole, as it sets the framework for numerous policies at national level.

Many policy proposals by the European Commission still are dominated by a particular focus on the achievement of the single market objective. This leads to an emphasis on striving to further implement the internal market by fighting any kind of 'distortion of competition' among enterprises from different Member States. Within this, however, the different characteristics of diverse enterprises are not yet accounted for very much. The social economy is still dealt with the same way as other enterprises, without taking into account additional costs they might bear and the added value they deliver, either as a primary result of the production or through an internalisation of costs that would otherwise have to be borne by society and that are most often not generated by the social economy, but by shortcomings of the economic system.

However, recently, a number of policy initiatives targeting the social economy in a direct or indirect way have been presented at European level. This increased interest in and engagement with the social economy or social business does not necessarily follow the same motivation, and there are three perspectives that are reflected in these policy initiatives:

- An increasing number of policy-makers have discovered and now clearly recognise the added societal value of the social economy (not least now in times of crisis) and wish to facilitate its development through the improvement of legal frameworks and access to finance;
- Others have the objective of encouraging more responsible behaviour of economic actors in general, by sanctioning or rewarding the performance of enterprises with regard to the impact they have on their environment;

- Some, however, also seem – more or less consciously – to wish to open 'new market opportunities' in the social sector for business in general.

Some examples of recent policy initiatives having an impact on the social economy will be presented below.

THE EUROPEAN PARLIAMENT RESOLUTION ON THE SOCIAL ECONOMY

Since the late 1980s, the issue 'social economy/social enterprise' appeared on – and again off – the EU agenda several times.

A milestone for the recognition of the role of the social economy was the European Parliament's (2009) *Resolution on Social Economy.*[95] With this resolution, the social economy received the support of the only EU institution that is directly elected and which, with the entry into force of the *Lisbon Treaty*, gained significant weight in the EU decision-making process. The resolution calls for a recognition of the concept of social economy and the added value it delivers. It suggests, in addition to a number of other measures, an adaption of the legal framework that would take into account these benefits. In this way, the European Parliament does not necessarily advocate preferential treatment of the social economy *vis-à-vis* other types of enterprises. However, it expects policy-makers to take into consideration this added value, including (societal) costs that the social economy absorbs through its operations, and to create a true level playing field (equal treatment of the social economy and other enterprises).

An important instrument to ensure follow-up and continuation of the Parliament's resolution is the European Parliament's Intergroup on Social Economy. This informal working group gathers 48 MEPs from different political groups, who are interested in joint initiatives, to follow developments in the social economy sector through an exchange with stakeholders representing social economy and civil society at large.

The *Resolution on Social Economy* (European Parliament, 2009) became a reference document for a number of policy initiatives of the European Parliament, the European Commission and the consultative bodies. In particular, the European Economic and Social Committee[96] (EESC) and the

---

95 Known also as the *Toia Report*.

96 The EESC was established in 1957 and acts today as a consultative body of the European Union. It is the place for the so-called 'social dialogue', where different social and economic interest groups – trade unions, employers, social economy/civil society sector – have a formal say on EU legislative proposals. The committee has 344 members,

Committee of the Regions[97] (COR) had already undertaken initiatives for the social economy.

SOCIAL BUSINESS INITIATIVE

The Communication, *Social Business Initiative – Creating a Favourable Climate for Social Enterprises, Key Stakeholders in the Social Economy and Innovation* (European Commission, 2011a) at least partially could be considered a reply by the European Commission to the claims made by the European Parliament (2009) in the *Toia Report*. It was published on 25 October 2011 and has its origin in the Communication, *Towards a Single Market Act* (proposals 36 and 37) (European Commission, 2010b).

A positive sign for a more coherent approach by the Commission towards social economy/social enterprise is the fact that the proposal is the outcome of teamwork between three Directorate-Generals (DG Enterprise and Industry, DG Internal Market and DG Employment and Social Affairs).

The Commission lists 11 'key actions' for promoting social enterprises and social economy to take place by the end of 2012. These key actions concern different policy fields and include, for example, a proposal for a regulation on European social entrepreneurship funds; work on micro-credit and other initiatives aimed at enhancing access to finance; a mapping of social enterprises and the establishment of a database on existing labels and certifications for social entrepreneurship or training for local and national administrations (European Commission, 2011a).

According to *Social Business Initiative*, social enterprises are:

> Businesses providing social services and/or goods and services to vulnerable persons (access to housing, health care, assistance for elderly or disabled persons, inclusion of vulnerable groups, childcare, access to employment and training, dependency management); and/or
>
> Businesses with a method of production of goods or services with a social objective (...) but whose activity may be outside the realm of the provision of social goods or services (European Commission, 2011: 3).

---

nominated by national governments and appointed by the Council of the European Union for a renewable five-year term.

97 The CoR's role is to put forward local and regional points of view on EU legislation. It does so mainly by issuing reports ('opinions') on Commission proposals. The Commission, the Council and the Parliament must consult CoR before EU decisions are taken on matters concerning local and regional government (for example, on employment policy, the environment, education or public health). The committee has 344 members.

This definition includes social economy, but also enterprises that are not collective undertakings and that do not necessarily apply principles such as participation, co-operation, and limited distribution of profits. If one applies the first definition, the initiative will support any kind of enterprise providing social services.

Despite other proposals by the European Commission in which reference is made to social entrepreneurship and a specific proposal on corporate social responsibility (CSR), there is still some confusion about what type(s) of enterprise will be targeted, what direction initiatives will take, and who they will serve. This is evident in the discussions on *Social Business Initiative* and related proposals that are currently taking place in the European Parliament, the EESC or the COR.

Much will depend on the extent to which social economy, other economic actors and citizens in general will make themselves heard, as well as on the intention of Member States to promote the different degrees to which an undertaking may prove to be 'social'.

The European Commission shows itself open to discussions. In May 2012, it established a multi-stakeholder expert group (GECES) to provide advice and to consider the implementation of the 11 key actions proposed by *Social Business Initiative* (European Commission, 2011a).

EUROPEAN SOCIAL ENTREPRENEURSHIP FUNDS

Access to funding always has been an important issue for social enterprises, even though it is only one of the challenges facing many social enterprises in their daily operations.

With its proposal for a regulation on European Social Entrepreneurship Funds (EuSEFs),[98] announced in *Social Business Initiative* and published on 7 December 2011, the European Commission intends to promote an increase in different types of private investment in social enterprises. The objective is to award the label 'European Social Entrepreneurship Fund' to investment funds that specifically target these kinds of businesses, provided that managers of the funds adhere to a number of rules set out by the European Commission.

Some elements of the Commission proposal generated a debate at the EU level, and also in Member States: one key question is what proportion of their capital should future EuSEFs allocate to social enterprises? If it is 70%, as suggested by the European Commission, would there be any control and/or

---

98 http://ec.europa.eu/internal_market/investment/social_investment_funds_en.htm.

transparency regarding the use of the remaining part of the capital? In addition, should there be a threshold regarding the annual turnover of potential beneficiaries (the European Commission proposes a threshold of €50 million)? If so, how should investment-intense sectors, such as social housing or hospitals and research, be dealt with? Should EuSEFs deal only with 'professional' clients, as stipulated by the European Commission, or should retail investors also be able to contribute (the latter would open the label EuSEF also to a number of already existing investment funds playing an important role in delivering funding for social economy in several EU Member States)? Finally, would it not be appropriate also to ask fund managers to be transparent on the origin of investment funds in order to avoid undertakings benefiting from EuSEFs whose sources of finance are inconsistent with the general aims and ethical profile of the beneficiaries of investments?

Finally, but most importantly, discussions focus on the definition, by the European Commission, of the eligible undertaking. Even though some elements, such as use of profits or stakeholder involvement have been specified, the definition still allows for a large number of enterprises (which may be more or less social) to access investment by EuSEFs. Again, values, structures and ownership of enterprises are not a central element.

Social economy operators fear that they might lose credibility *vis-à-vis* private investors should there be any misuse of the funds by enterprises whose 'social objective' turns out to be a mask only. It is here that the problem of measuring social impact comes back on the EU agenda and will have to be addressed.

The European Parliament, as well as governments of the Member States, will have a central role to play in shaping the regulation. The EESC is finalising its opinion (rapporteur: Ariane Rodert) and already has highlighted a fact that a number of EU policy-makers do not seem to be aware of: that is, figures show that investment into social economy enterprises is much less risky than investment in traditional undertakings. A main challenge in the adoption and implementation of a regulation on European Social Entrepreneurship Funds thus is linked to the vision of social economy/social enterprise the European Commission and others are conveying to potential investors in their communications and statements on the issue.

REGIONAL POLICY

The important impact that EU regional policy has had (and could potentially have) on the social economy should not be underestimated. EU Structural

Funds have contributed to a significant extent to the development of social economy enterprises. The promotion of partnerships between social economy and other public and private actors by EU cohesion policy also has led to the development of local/regional policies across individual Member States, which also enables the sector to develop its potential in cooperation with other public and private players.

A strong element of this policy is the willingness of DG Regio[99] to engage in a permanent dialogue with stakeholders and to consult with them during the preparation of new policy proposals, such as those on the future EU cohesion policy (2014-2020), tabled in October 2011.

The proposals for the new programming phase, should they be accepted as such by the European Parliament and the Council, could improve further development opportunities for social economy.

First, promotion of social enterprises figures among the investment priorities of the European Social Fund (ESF), as well as of the European Regional Development Fund (ERDF).

Moreover, the European Commission intends to make stronger use of so-called global grants that allow national governments to entrust intermediary bodies at local and regional level with management and implementation of a part of the funds. In the past, social economy figured among the beneficiaries of (a part of) these grants and, in some cases, also among the intermediary bodies.

Another major opportunity for the social economy is the community-led local development approach. This approach, if used by the Member States, would allow local action groups (composed of different stakeholders) to jointly develop local development strategies and be able to use a combination of funds for the implementation of this strategy.

The partnership approach in the implementation of EU cohesion policy is central to the new policy proposals and received an even larger focus.

Another positive aspect is that the proposals for the future EU cohesion policy have been coupled for the first time with several complementary proposals concerning employment and social policy after 2013. The EU Programme on Social Change and Innovation, with its axis on micro-finance and social entrepreneurship, is part of this package.

Next to all these positive developments, it should be highlighted, however, that the adoption of these policies and their implementation will

---

99 EU regional policy, coordinated by Directorate General (DG) for Regional Policy has, among its mission, the pursuit of the objective of Art.174 of the *Treaty* to strengthen the economic, social and territorial cohesion of the Union.

depend to a large extent on the willingness of each national government to make use of these provisions.

CONCLUSIONS

Social economy/social enterprise figures higher on the EU policy agenda than ever before. The European Commission has launched a number of initiatives that will have a direct or indirect impact on the further development of the social economy – many of these are across different policy areas.

The concrete direction these initiatives will take finally and the impact they will have for social economy will depend on the extent to which the diverse policies and measures recognise different degrees to which enterprises contribute to the well-being of society. Concepts such as 'social business', 'social enterprise' and 'social economy' certainly should not be used as synonyms and clearly require further clarification.

Furthermore, strengthening the potential of the social economy necessitates an even stronger linkage across different policy fields, such as enterprise policy, regional policy and social policy.

A major opportunity has been brought about by the provisions of the *Lisbon Treaty*, which widens possibilities for the participation by citizens in policy-making at EU level. The European Parliament, for instance, considerably gained decision-making power and is in a position to promote or block policy initiatives and to supervise their implementation. Social economy operators and civil society at large have the occasion to make MEPs an ally – in the framework of the Social Economy Intergroup and beyond.

Yet, considering all these developments, one should not forget about the key role national governments (the Council) play in adopting and implementing EU policies. It remains to be seen how far they are willing to promote the social economy, with a long-term view of fostering (socially) sustainable development, not just using the social economy as a 'fire extinguisher' in times of crisis. Social economy actors and civil society in general need to raise their voice *vis-à-vis* members of national parliaments in their city/region.

Finally, the development of the social economy will be determined by the degree to which policy-makers are ready to give local/regional authorities enough room for manoeuvre to make their choices and to build partnerships with those actors that show themselves able to contribute to the development and realisation of sustainable policies and strategies at local level.

12 Co-operatives – what relevance now?

Bridget Carroll,
Olive McCarthy and
Mary O'Shaughnessy

INTRODUCTION

Stiglitz (2009) argues that, in light of the monumental failure of financial institutions in recent years, we need to better understand the balance between private rewards and social returns. Co-operatives attempt to achieve this balance through open membership, democratic decision-making and equitable distribution of surpluses.[100] Their dual nature as businesses and voluntary associations situates them as potential agents of economic democracy, a central theme of this book.

This chapter presents an overview of co-operatives in Ireland by type and analyses aspects of their performance to date. It addresses some challenges that the co-operative sector in Ireland faces. The chapter also discusses the relationship between co-operatives, social enterprises more generally and related policy.

THE CURRENT STATUS OF CO-OPERATIVES IN IRELAND

While not defined in law, co-operatives in Ireland traditionally have registered as co-operative societies under the *Industrial and Provident Societies Acts, 1893-2005* and the *Credit Union Act, 1997*. However, co-operatives also can use other forms of incorporation, such as the company structure.[101] Since 2004, data on the sector has deteriorated considerably, as the Registry of Friendly Societies no longer reports the total number of members, sales/income, employees and assets of societies.[102]

Table 1 shows the total number of industrial and provident societies and credit unions at the end of 2010, which totalled 1,468.

---

100 The *Principles of Co-operation*, as agreed by the International Co-operative Alliance (an NGO representing co-operatives worldwide), are based on open and voluntary membership, democratic member control, limited returns on capital, distribution of profits as well as autonomy and independence, education, co-operation among co-operatives and concern for community.

101 The Registrar of Friendly Societies (RFS) does not differentiate between co-ops and other industrial and provident societies under the legislation but, according to the Registrar's 2010 report "most" of the industrial and provident Societies "are co-operative societies". Data collection on smaller sectors, such as worker co-ops, is hampered by the lack of classification for these sectors.

102 This is probably due to the fact that the Registry has been *de facto* amalgamated with the Companies Registration Office and scaled down in terms of staff.

Table 1: Co-operatives by type, Republic of Ireland, 2010

Co-op by type	Number
Agriculture, forestry, fishing & food	319
Credit unions[103]	405
Housing	50
Group Water Schemes	367
Promotion & Development	145
Other	182
Total	**1,468**

Sources: Registry of Friendly Societies, 2011; ILCU, 2011.

The total number of co-operatives (societies plus credit unions) increased by 116 from 1,352 to 1,468 from 1995 to 2010. However, the total number of new registrations has averaged at about 30 societies over the last number of years, down from 40 per year in the past. There has been a significant number of mergers among co-operatives in recent years – for example, between group water schemes and livestock marts. Transfers of engagements[104] between credit unions also have become more common, with a total of 18 having taken place since 2006. Analysis of Registry records for the last 10 years indicates that new co-operatives are emerging in the areas of environmental services, utilities and agriculture and food. In the next section, we will briefly examine co-operatives in Ireland by type.[105]

AGRICULTURAL CO-OPS[106]

The strength of the agricultural co-op sector is apparent from figures published by the Irish Co-operative Organisation Society (ICOS, 2010).[107] Total sectoral turnover for 2008[108] increased slightly to €12.7bn from €12.6bn

---

103 395 affiliated to the Irish League of Credit Unions (ILCU) and 11 affiliated to the Credit Union Development Association (CUDA), with overlapping membership of one credit union.

104 Where one credit union transfers its entire operations to another.

105 Co-operatives commonly are classified as producer, consumer or worker co-ops and, more recently, social or multi-stakeholder co-ops. In this chapter, co-ops are classified according to their designation by the RFS, with the addition of worker co-ops which are not classified on a separate basis by the RFS.

106 The agriculture category includes both productive and distributive societies in dairying, meat processing, livestock sales, livestock breeding, egg and poultry, horticulture, fishing, farm relief services and forestry as well as turf co-ops.

107 ICOS is a co-operative umbrella organisation.

108 In the co-operative dairy and mart societies.

in 2007. In particular, the dairy/multipurpose co-operatives have grown in strength over the past century and are contributing significantly to the development of an export industry. Irish agri-sector exports totalled approximately €8.9bn in 2008 (DAFF, 2010a), representing a contribution to gross domestic product of 6.6% in 2007 (DAFF, 2009).[109]

The performance of Irish farmer co-operatives to date has led to an established presence on the global market. However, that environment faces uncertainty. Changes in the agricultural policies of the European Union, combined with structural changes at the processor and retail levels, have resulted in co-operatives adopting a range of strategic responses to addressing the changing demands of the agribusiness environment (Ward, 2007). For instance, dairy co-ops in Ireland are currently preparing a response to the imminent lifting of EU milk quotas and increased milk output of 50% by 2020 under government policy as outlined in *Food Harvest 2020* (DAFF, 2010b).[110] This will likely see further restructuring in the sector in the coming years, including a large increase in milk processing capacity. New co-operatives of farmers in the dry-stock sector, in particular, are beginning to emerge, focusing on quality, environmental concerns and animal welfare and with a view to accessing premium markets and higher returns.

CREDIT UNIONS

The Irish League of Credit Unions has 395 affiliated credit unions in the Republic of Ireland, serving 2.65 million members, with savings of €10.7bn and loans of €5.03bn (ILCU, 2011). ILCU-affiliated credit unions in the Republic of Ireland have total assets of €12.4bn (ILCU, 2011) and an estimated 10,000 volunteers and 3,000 staff. The Credit Union Development Association (CUDA) represents an additional 11 affiliated credit unions, with some overlapping membership with the ILCU.[111]

Credit unions face significant challenges at present, with declining income and rising costs. Since 2008,[112] lending has decreased from 50% to 40% of total assets and arrears have increased from 6.5% of total lending to almost 17.6%. Loan write-offs increased by 29% between 2010 and 2011. This has hindered

---

109 This includes those dairy/multipurpose co-operatives that have taken a public limited company (PLC) route to raise finance for this growth.

110 This report outlines "a cohesive roadmap for the industry…".

111 There are an additional 103 ILCU-affiliated credit unions in Northern Ireland, as well as 77 credit unions affiliated to the Ulster Federation, the Tyrone Federation or operating independently (ILCU, 2011; DETI, 2009-2010).

112 All figures quoted here relate to ILCU-affiliated credit unions, for which reliable data is publicly available from the ILCU *Annual Report 2011* (ILCU, 2011).

the ability of credit unions to pay dividends to their savers, with the average dividend paid in 2011 being only 1.11%. However, this is not solely a result of declining income but also is caused by a focus on addressing solvency issues, increasing bad debt provisions and increasing reserves. Transfers of engagements from weaker credit unions to stronger credit unions are in greater evidence and this is a trend that is likely to grow over the coming years.

In 2011, the government established a Commission on Credit Unions to inform the preparation of new credit union legislation and to make recommendations on strengthening the regulation and governance framework of credit unions. The *Final Report of the Commission on Credit Unions* (2012) made a range of recommendations for restructuring of the credit union movement with a view, perhaps, to reducing the number of credit unions in the short to medium term. It also sought a strengthened regulatory framework for credit unions and a new governance standard. However, it should be noted that, like co-operative banks across the world, credit unions have fared better in economic crisis than the conventional banking sector. Credit unions now form the only remaining mutual banking sector in Ireland.

WORKERS' CO-OPERATIVES

The workers' co-op sector in Ireland is a small, fragmented sector. It is estimated that there are only 19 workers' co-operatives in Ireland (Gavin, 2012). This is a significant reduction from 1998, when there were 82 workers' co-ops on record. Current estimates put their turnover at €7.9m, wages at €3.3m[113] and total employees of 135 (Gavin, 2012). Workers' co-ops in Ireland are involved in food production, retailing and catering, printing, crafts, education and research, taxis and the arts.

Many reasons have been proposed for the lack of progress of workers' co-ops in general, including the lack of familiarity with the concept, the perception that investor-owned firms are more profitable and efficient, workers' inability to supply enough initial capital, cultural inertia and the existing dominant economic form being so heavily supported (Gunn, 2006). Alternatively, workers may prefer to make use of trade unions or political action to defend their interests rather than choosing the worker co-op model to achieve similar aims (MacPherson, 2000).

---

113 This figure may be underestimated, as some members act as self-employed members of the co-ops.

HOUSING CO-OPERATIVES

The co-operative housing movement in Ireland comprises 50 not-for-profit co-operative housing societies (Registry of Friendly Societies, 2011). The majority of housing co-operatives in Ireland are home ownership co-operatives, although the number of rental co-operatives has increased in recent years. Housing co-op schemes are supported under the Capital Assistance Scheme (CAS) and the Capital Loan and Subsidy Scheme (CLSS) of the Department of the Environment, Community and Local Government (DoECLG). The current economic and financial crisis has seen a withdrawal of most direct capital funding to the housing co-op sector. National housing policy now supports the leasing of properties as the main model of promoting social housing support. The National Association of Building Co-operatives (NABCo) estimates that new housing co-operative developments are likely to come from existing unfinished housing estates and it is currently piloting a number of such projects (O'Keeffe, 2012).

Group Water Schemes

Across Ireland, 367 group water schemes are registered as co-operative societies and are responsible for the supply of piped water to over 50,000 households (Registry of Friendly Societies, 2011), although some may be co-ops in name only (Forfás, 2007). The majority of schemes are affiliated to the National Federation of Group Water Schemes,[114] which has nine full-time employees. The schemes are largely funded through State subsidies under the Rural Water Programme and training grants from the DoECLG). The Group Water Scheme co-op sector has grown considerably as informal schemes incorporate.

Promotional and development co-operatives

This category includes a broad range of societies, including multi-stakeholder local development vehicles or 'community co-ops', often located in Gaeltacht[115] areas, co-ops that organise cultural and heritage events such as fairs, shows, festivals and museums, leisure and sports co-ops and tourism co-ops. As of 2004, there were 192 of these societies, representing over 14,000 members, with sales in excess of €7m and assets in excess of €23m. The number of these co-ops had decreased to 145 by 2010 (Registry of Friendly Societies, 2011). While there is no umbrella body for these co-ops *per se*,

---

[114] www.nfgws.ie.

[115] Officially designated as Irish-speaking areas.

Udarás na Gaeltachta[116] provides financial support for community co-operatives located within the regions it serves to a total budget of €1.96m in 2011. Few of the co-operative recipients of this funding would be likely to survive without this significant financial support. The community co-operatives in these Gaeltacht areas have established Comhlachas na gComharchumann, an umbrella body of which the co-operative managers are members.

Having examined co-operatives in Ireland by type, the achievement of co-ops in Ireland will be discussed in the next section.

ASSESSING THE ACHIEVEMENT OF CO-OPERATIVES IN IRELAND

While the co-operative movement has many intellectual and practical roots, not all of which see co-ops as having a role in transforming society, the visions and actions of many founders were often radical, aiming to address social injustice by promoting co-operatives beyond that of solutions to immediate needs or operating in any one sector of the economy.

Has the co-operative movement in Ireland lived up to this vision? Arguably, while the vision of many of the founders may have been radical, the resultant *organisation* tends to become conservative (Schwabenland, 2006). This can occur as the organisation concentrates its efforts on its 'core business', particularly as operations and administration of services tend to become more complex over time and as membership grows. The character of the co-operative as a social entity is thus weakened and, ultimately, this can lead to a lessening of the intellectual rigour of co-operativism (MacPherson, 2008).

Co-ops, along with other civil society organisations, are presumed to have a role in "common good outcomes" (Fairbairn, 2004: 305) including the promotion of social cohesion and as "schools of citizenship" but they are prone to the same environmental and institutional pressures as other organisations. The considerable time, effort and leadership needed for the co-operative process also may be underestimated and the presence of both social and economic goals is seen as both complementary and conflicting (Fairbairn, 2004). In short, it is probably unwise to idealise co-operatives.

Co-ops traditionally have been locally-based single stakeholder organisations established to serve their members' needs and thus focusing on a particular set of activities (although, more recently, multi-stakeholder

[116] The regional authority responsible for the economic, social and cultural development of the Gaeltacht.

models have been developed). This conception of co-ops disavows the notion that they form a 'movement' at all.

THE CHALLENGES FACING CO-OPERATIVES IN IRELAND TODAY

Taking a national view of the role of co-operatives, collaboration between co-operative sectors has been lacking.[117] As has occurred in other countries, it is often only when taxation or legislative issues arise that the sectors work together (MacPherson, 2000). Collaboration at national level is unlikely to develop if members, directors and staff as well as policy-makers do not have a sense of co-operatives having a distinct and clearly articulated value system and if the role of co-operatives in the community is not debated (International Joint Project on Co-operative Democracy, 1995). The lack of national collaboration displays a lack of deep commitment to co-operativism, as well as a lack of leadership within the movement, and arguably has led to a lack of visibility of the movement (MacPherson, 2000). Internationally, co-ops have significantly developed the promotional and communications aspects of their work in recent years.

However, while some may deride co-ops for narrowing their goals or for becoming 'too commercial', the significant impact of co-operatives in Ireland has yet to be thoroughly assessed. While the concentration of power and ownership in Irish society has been heavily criticised (TASC,[118] 2010), the co-operative model has helped to distribute wealth more equally across society. However, its full potential and promise has yet to be realised in Ireland (McCarthy *et al.*, 2010). A Forfás (2007) report suggested that co-operatives could play a greater role in Ireland, particularly in a social context, citing healthcare, housing and environmental protection. Problems faced by co-ops include a lack of visibility and an outdated legislative and regulatory environment. There is also a lack of support for new and emerging groups wishing to establish co-ops that do not fit under the remit of the existing representative bodies.[119]

---

117 The Forum for the Co-operative Movement in Ireland was established in 2005 in response to perceived challenges facing the movement and to anticipated reform of the legislative and regulatory framework for co-ops. However, the Forum has been inactive for some time.

118 TASC is as an independent think-tank concerned with economic inequality.

119 The Co-operative Development Society offers some support to emerging co-ops and Co-operative Support Services is a relatively new player on the field – offering support and advice to ethnic minorities developing co-ops.

An important question is whether the co-operative remains a relevant organisational form today or whether the values espoused by co-ops find other methods of expression and how these expressions ultimately compare in terms of delivery. Co-operatives face both challenges and opportunities in articulating their role(s) in society in the context of growing interest in social enterprise more generally. The next section of this chapter explores the relationship between co-operatives and social enterprise.

CO-OPERATIVES AND SOCIAL ENTERPRISE

Defourny and Nyssens (2006) have traced the European emergence of the concept of social enterprise to the early 1990s, following an impetus that was first Italian, linked closely with the co-operative movement, and cite the decision of the Italian parliament in 1991 to adopt a law creating a specific legal form for social co-operatives as the first formal appearance of European social enterprises (Defourny and Nyssens, 2006: 4). Borzaga and Santuari (1998) describe these social enterprises as co-operatives that arose primarily to respond to needs that had been inadequately met, or not met at all, by public services. In essence, social enterprises are argued to assume a plurality of roles, including advocacy and the provision of goods and services, and emerge to serve the community and/or community of interest.

Similar to co-operatives, social enterprises usually operate a 'one member, one vote' principle to ensure that control is not distributed according to share capital.[120] This democratic feature of the social enterprise is complemented by its efforts to ensure representation by all stakeholders, including the end-users and producers of the services produced. Defourny and Nyssens (2006: 6) argue that social enterprises attach themselves to certain co-operative principles and, consequently, the choice of registering as a co-operative or other type of limited profit legal entity is more likely dependent on legal mechanisms provided by national legislation.

Defourny and Nyssens (2006) also note that, in contrast to traditional co-operatives, social enterprises may be seen as more orientated to the whole community and as putting more emphasis on general interest.[121] Consequently, we can note the growing European trend for co-operatives

---

[120] The typical legal structure adopted is a company limited by share or guarantee.

[121] However, they caution overestimation of these contrasting differences, suggesting that the term 'social enterprises' can be regarded as constituting a new dynamic within the third sector.

and other social enterprises[122] to take over and improve the quality of services previously provided directly by the State, by religious institutions or by investor-driven businesses, as well as to provide services that are not readily available in local communities.

The Italian experiences, briefly mentioned already, stand out in this regard. For instance, by the late 1980s, a number of new social co-operatives had emerged in Italy in response to the perceived exclusion of certain groups from the mainstream labour market. In addition to this goal of work integration, social co-operatives also evolved to provide care-based services (Nyssens, 2006). The significance of this was reflected in the adoption of new legislation by the Italian Parliament in 1991, which created a particular legal form described as 'social solidarity co-operatives' (subsequently renamed 'social co-operatives')[123]. There were an estimated 7,400 of these co-ops in existence by 2005 (ISTAT, 2008).

The increased recognition of the role of social enterprises as a strategy for European economic growth is also evident in the *Single Market Act* (European Commission, 2011c), which defines social entrepreneurship and the social economy "as one out of 12 levers to create a new growth agenda in areas like social service, social work and work integration, but also in areas of climate change, quality food and access to scarce resources" (EMES, 2011).

Thus, in an Irish context, and against the backdrop of the current economic recession, reduced delivery of public services and growing levels of unemployment, the Irish government and other agents have demonstrated a re-invigorated interest in the social economy and social enterprises as a way of meeting community needs and stimulating the local economy. This is evident in statements such as that of Clann Credo and the Dublin Employment Pact (2010) in the *Report of the Social Enterprise Task Force* (SETF, 2010: 6) when they insist that "the social enterprise sector has the potential to develop to the level and scale that has been achieved in other countries".

---

122 Social enterprises in this context are understood as value-based organisations that operate for social, as well as financial, profit. They (1) use a variety of resources, including income-generating activities (trading), as well as (2) resources from civil society, such as volunteers, donations, etc. and (3) resources from the statutory sector in the form of public subsidies, subsidised employment grants, contracts, etc.; (4) they are participatory by nature, typically not-for-profit with democratic governance structures and (5) they actively engage in the provision of training and employment opportunities for those at risk of social exclusion.

123 The law distinguishes between two types of social co-operative: those delivering social, health and educational services, called 'A-type social co-operatives' (*co-operative sociali di tipo a*), and those providing work integration for disadvantaged people, referred to as 'B-type social co-operatives' (*co-operative sociali di tipo b*).

However, there is also the clear recognition that, to realise this, "the sector needs an appropriate national policy framework, access to relevant support structures and access to capital" (SETF, 2010: 1). This reflects the growing acknowledgement of the under-development of the sector in general and "a lack of policy focus and direction at national level (SETF, 2010: 1). Thus, in a period of sustained national economic recession in Ireland, it is imperative that we have a discussion on the appropriate policy support for the future development of Irish social enterprises, (Curtis *et al.*, 2011).

THE POLICY CONTEXT FOR CO-OPERATIVES

In terms of policy developments specifically for co-ops, the government has recently identified the co-operative model as:

> ... one of a number of legal options that are available to those considering establishing themselves in business (DJEI, 2012: 64)

and promises to:

> ... work to promote a greater appreciation of the co-operative model as a distinct form of organisation, ensure a level playing field between co-operatives and the other legal options for structuring enterprise activities, and provide a conducive framework for the full potential of the co-operative model to be realised, including in areas such as childcare, education, housing, energy retrofitting, environmental protection, transport and healthcare (Government of Ireland, 2011).

A programme of regulatory review and reform of the *Industrial and Provident Societies Acts* has been underway for some time. Some believe that the continued growth and development of the co-operative model in Ireland requires defining co-operatives within the existing or new acts and/or giving recognition to the distinct characteristics of co-operatives in Irish law.

The development of a coherent policy and legislative environment for the broader social economy sector would help contribute to the realisation of the potential the sector has to offer. Further engagement between co-operatives and other social enterprise actors also might be beneficial in terms of identifying common ground in the realisation of policy and sector development.

CONCLUSIONS

The co-operative movement is identified as an important strand of, and historical influence on, the development of the broader 'third sector' in Ireland (Donoghue and Larragy, 2009). Co-ops have developed a distinct approach to dealing with surplus and generating collective wealth rather than return on individual investment (Evers and Laville, 2004, citing Borgaza and Defourny, 2001). The co-op structure allows groups to trade, distribute surplus, raise capital and make incremental increases in resources. As such, the co-operative structure is as relevant as ever. The scope of activities being undertaken by co-operatives demonstrates the versatility of the model but there are many sectors in which the model does not appear in Ireland. However, co-operatives in Ireland need to address the relatively low visibility of the sector, the limited support services available for co-ops and the legal and regulatory environment.

Society needs organisational models and processes that distribute goods and services and resources in an equitable and efficient way. Some will seek transformative models in the 'solidarity economy'; others will seek instrumental or pragmatic solutions to shared problems. There is potential therefore for further development of co-operatives and social enterprises and this could be enhanced with greater engagement between existing co-operatives and other social enterprises in the creation of a better overall environment for these important organisations.

Conclusions – the way forward for social enterprise

It could be perceived from the preceding chapters in this book that social enterprise as a concept or as a driver of economic regeneration is undervalued and poorly understood – amongst policy-makers, the State and amongst communities in Ireland. Where it has been understood by policy-makers, it has been designated as little more than what Pearce regarded as a sector whose primary role is to facilitate labour market State objectives. Hence, social enterprise is under-developed in Ireland, relative to other countries – in terms of practice, policy and, indeed, ideology.

Chapters in this book have illustrated the benefits of social enterprise in specific sectors – for example, from renewable energy and wider green economy initiatives, in countries such as Denmark, to housing and regeneration in the UK. Such initiatives can benefit local communities, but also wider interests, such as the State. For example, community energy initiatives can support the State in achieving its renewable energy targets, and community regeneration led by voluntary housing associations can offer an alternative to Public Private Partnerships and existing models of regeneration.

We have also seen how social enterprise can empower communities of interest: the case study of Galway Traveller Movement shows how social enterprise development can achieve outcomes that the State and the private sector are ill-equipped or unwilling to achieve. Social enterprise can support economic self-determination, and so can contribute to greater equality for communities that either have been discriminated against, such as Travellers, or who have been neglected by the State and the private sector, and where needs of communities are not being met.

We argue that the benefits to the State (and to Irish society as a whole) need to be fully understood, and social enterprise needs to be part of the way we do business. It is not simply a labour market mechanism, but a way to achieve greater inclusion and equality in Ireland, through greater economic self-determination in communities.

Chapters 1 and **2** highlighted some of the different ideological perspectives of social enterprise. Communities need to have an understanding of the radical, reformist, and social entrepreneurship perspectives. Otherwise, social enterprise potentially could be an instrument of neo-liberal policies rather than an alternative to them.

If there is little consciousness amongst the mainstream about social enterprise, perhaps it is because the sector and its potential to date has not been widely articulated, or promoted. And the only way this can be addressed is by the sector itself. Social enterprises must articulate their concerns, vision and demands, and communicate and engage with the private and public sectors, as well as with the community and voluntary sector as a whole. There is a lack of cohesion in the sector in Ireland and this needs to be addressed.

While social enterprises may not have flourished so far in Ireland in comparison to European countries, there is no reason to assume that this will be the case always. Ireland has a strong history of social economy organisations and collective action, noted by such organisations as the GAA, the agricultural co-operative movement, and the credit union movement, the last being the world's largest (*per capita*) financial co-operative.

When such organisations were first established, they were not always met with support: when Horace Plunkett resigned from his post in the Department of Agriculture in 1907, his successor, Thomas Wallace Russell, referred to credit societies as "rotten and indefensible". His belief was that "this idea of people lending to one another their own money, was almost immoral ... it was depriving some unfortunate bankers of the opportunity of making a profit ... it was a preposterous thing to have these ignorant peasants dealing in financial matters".

The existence of a strong 'social economy' in Ireland, such as the credit union movement and agricultural co-operative sector, points to an infrastructure that may need to be called upon to engage with and support the emergence of social enterprises. After all, three of the seven principles of co-operation:[124] education, training and information; co-operation among co-operatives; and concern for community have a direct relevance to support and engagement with social enterprises.

There are other reasons to be positive, particularly with the EU Commission's *Social Business Initiative* (2011a) as well as commitments given in the *Programme for Government* (Government of Ireland, 2011). These commitments need to be followed up by concrete supports, which – as **Chapter 4** highlights – should be delivered at local level by the social enterprise sector. Just as the State views the private sector and acknowledges its role in facilitating private sector development, so too must it acknowledge the role of social enterprise. However, although social enterprise has many strengths, it is not a substitute for a progressive welfare state.

It is now incumbent on social enterprises and the wider social economy to play their part in ensuring that social enterprise has the same impact that agricultural co-operatives and the credit union movement have had – and continue to have – in communities in Ireland. This could lead to communities throughout the country having greater level of economic self-determination,

---

124 International Co-operative Alliance (ICA) specifies seven principles of co-operation as guidelines by which co-operatives put their values into practice.

thereby reducing the spectre of emigration, unemployment, alienation and isolation.

Bibliography

All Ireland Traveller Health Study Team (AITHS) (2010). *All Ireland Traveller Health Study*, Dublin: Department of Health and Children.

Amin, A. (2005). 'Local Community on Trial', *Economy and Society*, Vol.34, No.4, pp. 612-633.

Amin, A. (2009). 'Locating the Social Economy', in Amin, A. (ed.), *The Social Economy – International Perspectives on Economic Solidarity*, London: Zed Books.

Amin, A., Cameron, A. and Hudson, R. (2002). *Placing the Social Economy*, London: Routledge.

Anthony Collins Solicitors (2006). *The Scope for Using Social Clauses in UK Public Procurement to Benefit the UK Manufacturing Sector: A Report for the Manufacturing Forum*, London: Department of Trade and Industry

Anthony Collins Solicitors and MacFarlane, R. (2007). *Targeted Recruitment & Training Toolkit (Construction)*, Newcastle: Tyne & Wear Collaborative Efficiency Programme.

Anthony Collins Solicitors and MacFarlane, R. (2010): *Targeted Recruitment and Training Toolkit (Resource 2b Procurement: The Legal Framework for UK Public Bodies)*, Newcastle: North East Improvement and Efficiency Partnership.

Bank of England (2003). *The Financing of Social Enterprise: A Special Report by the Bank of England*, London: Domestic Finance Division, Bank of England.

Barry, M. and Chapman, R. (2009). 'Distributed Small-scale Wind in New Zealand: Advantages, Barriers and Policy Instruments', *Energy Policy*, Vol.37, pp.3358-3369.

Bishop, M. and Green, M. (2008). *Philanthrocapitalism – How the Rich Can Save the World and Why We Should Let Them*, London: AC Black.

Bolger, P. (1977). *The Irish Co-operative Movement*, Dublin: Institute of Public Administration.

Bolinger, M. (2001). *Community Wind Power Ownership Schemes in Europe and their Relevance to the United States*, Berkeley, CA: Lawrence Berkeley National Laboratory.

Borzaga, C. and Defourny, J. (eds.) (2001). *The Emergence of Social Enterprises*, London: Routledge.

Borzaga, C. and Santuari, A. (eds.) (1997). *Servizi Sociale e Nuova Occupazione: L'esperienza delle Nuove Figure di Imprenditorialita Sociale in Europa*, Vol.1, Trento: Regione Trentino Alto-Adige.

Byrne, A., Rush, M. and Yeates, N. (1999). *The Whole-Time Jobs Initiative: Processes of Exclusion and Integration*, Dublin: Combat Poverty Agency and Dublin Inner City Partnership.

Campbell, V. (2012). 'The Irish Procurement Landscape', presentation by Vincent Campbell, Director, National Procurement Service, Alexander Hotel, Dublin, 16 February 2012.

Caron, D.C. (2003). 'Cities, States, and Foreign Affairs: The Massachusetts Burma Case and Beyond: The Structure and Pathologies of Local Selective Procurement Ordinances: A Study of the Apartheid-Era South Africa Ordinances', *Berkeley Journal of International Law*, Vol.21, p.159.

Central Bank of Ireland (2006). *Guidance Note on Investments*, Dublin: Central Bank of Ireland.

Central Statistics Office (CSO) (2012). *Census 2011*, Cork: Central Statistics Office.

Chapman, T., Forbes, D. and Brown, J. (2007). 'They Have Good on their Side: The Impact of Public Sector Attitudes on the Development of Social Enterprise', *Social Enterprise Journal*, Vol.3, No.1, pp.78-89.

Clancy, P. and Murphy, G. (2006). *Outsourcing Government – Public Bodies and Accountability*, Dublin: TASC/New Island.

Clann Credo and Dublin Employment Pact (2010). *Adding Value, Delivering Change: The Role of Social Enterprise in National Recovery*, Dublin: Clann Credo and Dublin Employment Pact.

Clarke, A. and Eustace, A. (2009). *Exploring Social Enterprise in Nine Areas in Ireland*, Dublin: PLANET.

ClientEarth (2011a). *Clarifying the Link to the Subject Matter for Sustainable Procurement Criteria*, Legal briefing No.4, October, London: ClientEarth.

ClientEarth (2011b). *Identifying Opportunities for Sustainable Public Procurement: Specific Conditions*, Legal briefing No. 8, October, London: ClientEarth.

Cohen, J. and Rogers, J. (1995). 'Secondary associations and democratic governance', in Wright, E.O. (ed.), *Associations and Democracy*, London: Verso.

Cole, G.D.H. (1920). *Guild Socialism Restated*, London: Routledge.

Colvin, C. and McLaughlin, E. (2012). 'Raiffeisenism Abroad: Why Did German Microfinance Fail in Ireland but Prosper in the Netherlands?', European University Institute Max Weber programme Working papers (2012/01).

Comhar and Trinity College Dublin (2011). *Community Renewable Energy in Ireland*, Dublin: Comhar/Trinity College Dublin.

Commission on Credit Unions (2012). *Final Report of the Commission on Credit Unions*, Dublin: Stationery Office.

Coompanion (n.d.). *Co-operative Development in Sweden*, Stockholm: Coompanion.

Corbino, A. (2012). 'The Italian solidarity economy's slow revolution', *Grassroots Economic Organizing (GEO) Newsletter*, Vol.2, No.12, available at http://www.geo.coop/story/italian-solidarity-economy's-slow-revolution.

Cunningham, F. (2002). *Theories of Democracy*, London: Routledge.

Curtis, A., O' Shaughnessy, M. & Ward, M. (2011). 'An Examination of the Tensions and Challenges Associated with Operating as a Social Enterprise – the Case of Irish Social Enterprises', paper presented to the 3rd EMES International Research Conference on Social Enterprise, *Social Innovation through Social Entrepreneurship in Civil Society*, Roskilde (Denmark), July 2011, available at http://www.emes.net/index.php?id=538.

Daly, T. (1998). 'Area-based Strategies in Tallaght' in Fahy, K. (ed.), *Strategies to Develop the Social Economy*, Galway: Community Workers Co-op.

Defourny, J. and Nyssens, M. (2006). 'Defining Social Enterprises' in Nyssens, M. (ed.) *Social Enterprise: At the Crossroads of Market, Public Policies and Civil Society*, London: Routledge.

Defourny, J. and Nyssens, M. (2008). *Social Enterprise in Europe: Recent Trends and Developments*, Liège, Belgium: EMES European Research Network.

Department of Agriculture, Fisheries and Food (DAFF) (2009). *Annual Review and Outlook for Agriculture, Fisheries and Food 2008-2009*, Dublin: Stationery Office.

Department of Agriculture, Fisheries and Food (DAFF) (2010a). *Factsheet on Irish Agriculture,* accessed 14 June 2011 from http://www.agriculture.gov.ie/publications/2009/.

Department of Agriculture, Fisheries and Food (DAFF) (2010b). *Food Harvest 2020: A Vision for Irish Agri-food and Fisheries,* Dublin: Stationery Office.

Department of Communications, Energy and Natural Resources (DCENR) (2010). *National Renewable Energy Action Plan,* Dublin: Stationery Office.

Department of Communities and Local Government (2008). *National Procurement Strategy for Local Authorities,* London: HMSO.

Department of Enterprise, Trade and Investment (DETI) (2009-10). *Registry of Credit Unions and Industrial and Provident Societies Annual Report,* Belfast: Department of Enterprise, Trade and Investment.

Department of Finance (2010). *Circular 10/10: Guidance on Measures to Facilitate Participation of SMEs in Public Procurement,* Dublin: Stationery Office.

Department of Jobs, Enterprise and Innovation (DJEI) (2012). *Action Plan for Jobs 2012,* Dublin: Stationery Office.

Department of Public Expenditure and Reform and Department of Environment Community and Local Government (2012). *Green Tenders: An Action Plan on Green Public Procurement,* Dublin: Stationery Office.

Department of the Environment, Communities and Local Government (DoECLG) (2002). *Capital Funding Schemes for the Provision of Rental Accommodation by Approved Housing Bodies (Voluntary & Co-Operative Housing),* VHU 2/02, Dublin: Stationery Office.

Department of the Environment, Communities and Local Government (DoECLG) (2011). *Housing Policy Statement,* June, Dublin: Stationery Office.

Department of Trade and Industry (2002). *Social Enterprise – A Progress Report on Social Enterprise: A Strategy for Success,* London: HMSO.

Donoghue, F. and Larragy, J. (2009). 'Changing State-Civil Society Relationships in Ireland' in Gidron, B. & Bar, M. (eds.), *Policy Initiatives Towards the Third Sector in International Perspective,* New York: Springer.

Doyle, G. (2009). ' *What Difference Does It Make? The Current and Potential Contribution of Social Enterprises to the Regeneration of Urban Disadvantaged Communities in the Republic of Ireland'*, unpublished dissertation for MSc in Local Development, University of Glasgow.

Doyle, G. (2010). 'Social Enterprise: An Overlooked Approach to Addressing Economic Marginalisation', *Working for Change – The Irish Journal of Community Work,* second edition.

Doyle, G. and Lalor, T. (2010). *Social Enterprise – An Overlooked Approach to Promoting Sustainable Economic Regeneration,* Dublin: TASC.

Drudy, P.J. (1995). 'From Protectionism to Enterprise: A Review of Irish Industrial Policy' in Burke A. (ed.), *Enterprise and the Irish Economy,* pp. 71-89, Dublin: Oak Tree Press.

Drudy, P.J. and Punch, M. (2005). *Out of Reach: Inequalities in the Irish Housing System,* Dublin: TASC/New Island Books.

Edwards, M. (2009). 'Philanthrocapitalism: After the Goldrush', in Curzon Price, T. and Hayes, D. (eds.), *The Power of Giving – Philanthrocapitalism Debated*, London: Open Democracy.

EMES (2011). *Position Paper on the Social Business Initiative*, November, Liège, Belgium: EMES.

European Commission (1993). *Growth, Competitiveness and Employment: The Challenges and Ways Forward into the 21st Century*, Brussels: European Commission.

European Commission (2004). *Buying Green! A Handbook on Environmental Public Procurement*, staff working document, August, SEC(2004) 1050, Brussels: European Commission.

European Commission (2010a). *Buying Social: A Guide to Taking Account of Social Considerations in Procurement*, Brussels: DG Employment, Social Affairs and Equal Opportunities and DG Internal Market.

European Commission (2010b). *Towards a Single Market Act* (proposals 36 and 37), Brussels: European Commission.

European Commission (2011a). *Social Business Initiative: Creating a Favourable Climate for Social Enterprises, Key Stakeholders in the Social Economy and Innovation Economy and Innovation*, COM(2011) 682 final, Communication from the Commission to the European Parliament, the Council, the European Economic and Social Committee and the Committee of the Regions, available at http://ec.europa.eu/internal_market/ social_business/index_en.htm.

European Commission (2011b). *Towards a More Efficient European Procurement Market*, COM(2011) 15 final, Brussels, European Commission.

European Commission (2011c). *Single Market Act: Twelve Levers to Boost Growth and Strengthen Confidence: Working Together to Create New Growth*, COM(2011) 206 final, Communication from the Commission to the European Parliament, the Council, the Economic and Social Committee and the Committee of the Regions: Brussels, European Commission.

European Parliament (2009). *Resolution on Social Economy*, adopted 19 February, rapporteur: Patrizia Toia, Brussels: European Parliament, available at http://www.europarl.europa.eu/sides/getDoc.do?type= TA&reference=P6-TA-2009-0062&language=EN.

Evers, A. and Laville, J.L. (eds.) (2004). *The Third Sector in Europe*, Cheltenham: Edward Elgar.

Fairbairn, B. (2004). 'Setting New Directions' in Fairbairn, B. and Russell, N. (eds.), *Co-operative Membership and Globalization: New Directions in Research and Practice*, Saskatoon, Canada: Centre for the Study of Co-operatives, University of Saskatchewan, pp. 283-310.

Feasta (2007). *Envisioning a Sustainable Ireland from an Availability Perspective – A Report to the Environmental Protection Agency*, Dublin: Feasta.

Forfás (2007). *Ireland's Co-operative Sector*, Dublin: Forfás.

Forfás (2009). *Developing the Green Economy in Ireland: Report of the High Level Group on the Green Economy*, Dublin: Forfás.

Fraisse, L., Lhuillier, V. and Petrella, F. (2007). 'Une Proposition de Typologie des Régimes de Gouvernance à Partir des Évolutions Observées dans les Services d'Accueil des Jeunes Enfants en Europe, Working Papers Series, No. 07/01, Liège, Belgium: EMES European Research Network.

Friedmann, J. (1992). *Empowerment: The Politics of Alternative Development*, Cambridge: Blackwell.

Gallagher, S (2000). 'P.J. Meghan and Approved Local Councils: A Neglected Experiment in Community Development', in *Administration*, Vol. 48, No.2, pp.77-91.

Gavin, M. (2012). 'Ireland's Worker Co-operative Sector', unpublished MSc thesis, Department of Food Business and Development, University College Cork.

GHK (2006). *Social Enterprise – An International Literature Review*, London: Small Business Service.

Gibson-Graham, J.K. (2005). 'Surplus Possibilities: Postdevelopment and Community Economies, *Singapore Journal of Tropical Geography*, Vol.26, pp. 4-26.

Government of Ireland (2011). *Programme for Government*, Dublin: Stationery Office.

Grant Thornton (2009). *Strategic Review of the Capital Funding Schemes for Voluntary and Co-operative Housing*, Dublin: Centre for Housing Research.

Gunn, C. (2006). 'Co-operatives and Market Failure: Workers' Co-operatives and System Mismatch', *Review of Radical Political Economics*, Vol.38, pp.345.

Harvey, D. (2000). *Spaces of Hope*, Edinburgh: Edinburgh University Press.

Hastings, T., Sheehan, B. and Yeates, P. (2007). *Saving the Future: How Social Partnership Shaped Ireland's Economic Success*, Dublin: Blackhall Publishing.

Herlihy, N. (1969). 'Before the Dawn: Ideas and Events Leading to the Start of Credit Unions in Ireland', article published by Chapter 3 (Belfast area) of the Irish League of Credit Unions.

Hirst, P. (1989). *The Pluralist Theory of the State: Selected Writings of G.D.H. Cole, J.N. Figgis and H.J. Laski*, London: Routledge.

Hirst, P. (1994). *Associative Democracy: New Forms of Economic and Social Governance*, Cambridge: Polity Press.

Hirst, P. (1995). 'Can Secondary Associations Enhance Democratic Governance?', in Wright, E.O. (ed.), *Associations and Democracy*, London: Verso.

Hirst, P. (1997). *From Statism to Pluralism*, London: University College London Press.

HM Treasury (1999). *Enterprise and Social Exclusion*, London: HM Treasury.

Hoggett, R. (2000). *Community Owned Renewable Energy*, Camborne, Cornwall: Community Energy Plus.

Hutton, E. (2005). 'Scottish Strategy Needs More Focus', *Social Enterprise*, August, available at http://www.senscot.net/view_art.php?viewid=2904.

International Joint Project on Co-operative Democracy (1995). *Making Membership Meaningful: Participatory Democracy in Co-operatives*, Saskatchewan, Canada: Centre for the Study of Co-operatives, University of Saskatchewan.

International Monetary Fund (IMF) (2008). *World Economic Outlook: Housing and the Business Cycle*, Washington DC: International Monetary Fund.

Irish Co-operative Organisation Society (ICOS) (2010). *2009 Annual Report*, accessed 6 June from http://www.icos.ie/content/content.asp/ section_id=362.

Irish League of Credit Unions (ILCU) (2011). *Annual Report 2011*, Dublin, Irish League of Credit Unions.

Irwin, A. (2006). *Stall Anoishe! Minceirs Whiden Stop Here! Travellers Talking: Analysing the Reality for Travellers in Galway City,* Galway: Galway Traveller Movement.

ISTAT (2008). *Social Co-operatives in Italy – Year* 2005 (*Le co-operative sociali in Italia – Anno 2005),* Informazioni no.4, Roma: ISTAT.

Jackson, T. (2011). *Prosperity without Growth: Economics for a Finite Planet,* London: Earthscan.

Kennelly, J. (2011). 'The Irish Co-operative Movement', *Studies,* Vol. 100.

Kirby, P. (2002). *The Celtic Tiger in Distress: Growth with Inequality in Ireland,* Basingstoke: Palgrave.

LaMarche, G. (2009). 'Philanthropy for Social Change', in Curzon Price, T. and Hayes, D. (eds.). *The Power of Giving – Philanthrocapitalism Debated,* London: Open Democracy.

Lander, E. (2011). *The Green Economy: The Wolf in Sheep's Clothing,* Amsterdam: Transnational Institute.

Leyshon, A., Lee, R. and Williams, C. (2003). *Alternative Economic Spaces,* London: Sage.

Lyon, F. and Ramsden, M. (2006). 'Developing Fledging Social Enterprises? A Study of the Support Required and Means of Delivering It, *Social Enterprise Journal,* Vol.2, No.1, pp.27-41.

MacFarlane, R. and Cook, M. (2002). *Achieving Community Benefits through Contracts – Law, Policy and Practice,* Bristol: The Policy Press (for the Joseph Rowntree Foundation).

MacFarlane, R. and Cook, M. (2008). *Community Benefits in Public Procurement: A Report Demonstrating the Methodology for Including Targeted Recruitment and Training Clauses in Public Sector Contracts,* Edinburgh: The Scottish Executive, available at http://www.scotland.gov.uk/Resource/Doc/212427/ 0056513.pdf.

MacPherson, I. (2000). 'In These Pioneer Days: George Keen and Leadership through Sacrifice and Determination', in Fairbairn, B., MacPherson, I. and Russell, N. (eds.), *Canadian Co-operatives in the Year 2000: Memory, Mutual Aid and the Millennium,* Saskatoon, Canada: Centre for the Study of Co-operatives, University of Saskatchewan. pp.40-54.

MacPherson, I. (2008). 'Confluence, Context and Community: The Expanding Boundaries of Co-operative Studies' in MacPherson, I. and McLoughlin-Jenkins, E. (eds.), *Integrating Diversities within a Complex Heritage: Essays in the Field of Co-operative Studies,* Victoria, Canada: University of Columbia/New Rochdale Press, pp. 391-437.

Maegard, P. (2009). *Danish Renewable Energy Policy,* Bonn: World Council for Renewable Energy, available at http://www.wcre.de/en/images/stories/pdf/WCRE_Maegaard_Danish%20RE%20Policy.pdf.

McCarthy, O., Briscoe, R. & Ward, M. (2010). 'People in Control: The Promise of the Co-operative Business Approach', in Hogan, J., Donnelly, P.F. and O'Rourke, B.K. (eds.), *Irish Business and Society: Governing, Participating and Transforming in the 21st Century,* Dublin: Gill & Macmillan, pp.319-336.

Mcintosh, A. (2001). *Soil and Soul: People* versus *Corporate Power,* London: Aurum Press.

Mingione, E. (1991). *Fragmented Societies: A Sociology of Economic Life Beyond the Market Paradigm,* Oxford: Basil Blackwell.

Molloy, A., Mc Feely, C. and Connolly, E. (2000). *Building a Social Economy for the New Millennium*, Derry: Guildhall Press.

Morgan, G. (2004). 'Changing Capitalisms?', in Morgan, G., Whitley, R. and Moen, E. (eds.), *Changing Capitalisms? Internationalization, Institutional Change and Systems of Economic Organization,* Oxford: Oxford University Press.

Moulaert, F. and Ailenei, O. (2005). 'Social Economy, Third Sector and Solidarity Relations: A Conceptual Synthesis from History to Present, *Urban Studies,* Vol.42, pp.2037-2054.

National Economic and Social Forum (NESF) (2003). *The Policy Implications of Social Capital in Ireland,* Dublin: National Economic and Social Forum.

National Housing Federation (NHF) (2008). *Neighbourhood Audit 2008,* London: National Housing Federation.

New Economics Foundation (2002). *Plugging the Leaks: Making the Most of Every Pound that Enters Your Local Economy,* London: New Economics Foundation.

Nyssens, M. (ed.) (2006). *Social Enterprise: At the Crossroads of Market, Public Policies and Civil Society,* London and New York: Routledge.

Ó Broin, D. (2009). 'Institutionalising Social Partnership in Ireland', in Ó Broin, D. and Kirby, P. (eds.), *Power, Dissent and Democracy – Civil Society and the State in Ireland,* Dublin: A&A Farmar.

Ó Broin, D. and Waters, E. (2007). Governing Below the Centre: Local Governance in Ireland, Dublin: TASC/New Ireland.

O'Hearn, D. (2001). *The Atlantic Economy: Britain, the US and Ireland,* Manchester: Manchester University Press.

O'Keeffe, N. (2012). 'Co-operative Housing: Continuing to Deliver for Communities', in *CU Focus,* Spring.

O'Neill, P. M. (1997). 'Bringing the Qualitative State into Economic Geography' in: Lee, R. and Wills, J. (eds.), *Geographies of Economies,* pp.290-301, London: Arnold.

Office of the Third Sector (2008). *Social Clauses Project: Report,* London: HMSO.

O'Hanlon, G. (2010). 'A New Economic Paradigm?', *Working Notes,* Vol.63, pp.3-10.

Pahl, R., Flynn, R. and Buck, N. (1983). *Structures and Processes of Urban Life,* London: Longman.

Pearce, J. (1993). *At the Heart of the Community Economy: Community Enterprise in a Changing World,* London: Calouste Gulbenkien Foundation.

Pearce, J. (2003). *Social Enterprise in Anytown,* London: Calouste Gulbenkien Foundation.

Perera, O., Chowdhury, N. and Goswami, A. (2007). *State of Play in Sustainable Public Procurement,* Manitoba: International Institute for Sustainable Development.

Power, A. and Richardson, L. (1996). *Housing Plus: An Agenda for Social Landlords,* London: London School of Economics.

Prizeman, G. and Crossan, D. (2011). *Mapping Social Entrepreneurial Enterprises in Ireland,* Dublin: Initiative on Social Entrepreneurship, Centre for Nonprofit Management, Trinity College, Dublin, available at http://cnm.tcd.ie/assets/ pdf/sei-mapping-report.pdf.

Procurement Research Group, Faculty of Business, Dublin City University (2012): *Opportunities in Public Sector Procurement: The National Procurement Service Annual Survey 2012*, Dublin: Office of Public Works.

Putnam, R. (1993). *Making Democracy Work: Civic Traditions in Modern Italy*, Princeton: Princeton University Press.

Putnam, R. (2000). *Bowling Alone: The Collapse and Renewal of American Community*, Cambridge: Harvard University Press.

Quinn, A. (1999). *Credit Unions in Ireland*, Dublin: Oak Tree Press.

Registry of Friendly Societies (2011). *Report of the Registry of Friendly Societies 2010*, Dublin: The Stationery Office.

Schwabenland, C. (2006), *Stories, Visions and Values in Voluntary Organisations*, Aldershot: England, Ashgate.

Scottish Government (2007). *Better Business: A Strategy and Action Plan for Social Enterprise in Scotland*, Edinburgh: Scottish Government.

Shaw, E. (2004). 'Marketing in the Social Enterprise Context: Is It Entrepreneurial?', *Qualitative Market Research: An International Journal*, Vol.7, No.3, pp.194-205.

Slatter, P. (2001). *After the Crossroads – Housing Associations as Community Investors.* York: YPS.

Smallbone, D., Evans, M., Ekanem, I. and Butters, S. (2001). *Researching Social Enterprise*, Middlesex: Middlesex Business School, Middlesex University.

Social Enterprise Network Scotland (SENSCOT) (2009). *A Distinct Movement*, Edinburgh: Social Enterprise Network Scotland, available at http://www.senscot.net/view_art.php?viewid=7867.

Social Enterprise Task Force (SETF) (2010). *Adding Value, Delivering Change: The Role of Social Enterprise in National Recovery*, Dublin: Clann Credo and Dublin Employment Pact.

Social Justice Ireland (2012). *Shaping Ireland's Future*, Dublin: Social Justice Ireland.

Stiglitz, D.J. (2009). 'Moving Beyond Market Fundamentalism to a More Balanced Economy', *Annals of Public and Co-operative Economics*, Vol.80, Iss.3, pp.345-360.

Strategic Investment Board (2010). *Delivering Social Benefits through Public Procurement: A Toolkit*, Belfast: Strategic Investment Board.

Stryjan, Y. (2004). *Work integration social enterprises in Sweden*, WP No.04/02, Liège, Belgium: EMES.

Sustainable Energy Authority of Ireland (SEAI) (2010). *Renewable Energy in Ireland: Update*, Dublin: Sustainable Energy Authority of Ireland.

Sustainable Procurement Task Force (2006). *Procuring the Future – Sustainable Procurement National Action Plan: Recommendations from the Sustainable Procurement Task Force*, Dublin: Stationery Office.

TASC (2010). *Mapping the Golden Circle*, Dublin: TASC.

Task Force on the Traveller Community (1995). *Report*, Dublin: Stationery Office.

The Economist (2010) 'Let's Hear Those Ideas – A Social Innovation Briefing', 14 August.

Trybus, M. (2008). 'Social Clauses and EU Public Procurement', paper to the *International Conference on Corporate Social Responsibility, Business Responsibilities for*

Human Rights and International Law, Copenhagen University and Copenhagen Business School, 6-7 November.

TSA Consultancy (2003). *Social Finance in Ireland: What It Is and Where It's Going, with Recommendations for Its Future Development*, Dublin: Dublin Employment Pact, Westmeath Employment Pact, Clann Credo and ADM.

Unger, R.M. (2009). *The Left Alternative*, London: Verso.

Walker, G., Hunter, S., Devine-Wright, P., Evans, B. and Fay, H. (2007). 'Harnessing Community Energies: Explaining and Evaluating Community Based Localism in Renewable Energy Policy in the UK', *Global Environmental Politics*, Vol.7, pp.64-82.

Walsh, J. (1998). *Local Partnerships for Social Inclusion*, Dublin: Oak Tree Press.

Ward, M. (2007). 'Emerald Pastures', *Rural Co-operatives*, Vol.74, No.5 (Sept/Oct), pp.14-19.

Warren, M. (2001). *Democracy and Association*, Princeton: Princeton University Press.

Welsh Assembly Government (WAG) (2003). *Business Support and Needs of Social Economy Enterprises*, Cardiff: Welsh Assembly Government.

Wilkinson, R. and Pickett, K. (2009). *The Spirit Level: Why More Equal Societies Almost Always Do Better*, London: Allen Lane.

Wood, G. and Roper, I. (2004). 'Towards a Revitalisation of the Public', in Dibben, P,. Wood, G. and Roper, I. (eds.), *Contesting Public Sector Reforms – Critical Perspectives, International Debates*, Basingstoke: Palgrave Macmillan.

Index

Oak Tree Press

Oak Tree Press develops and delivers information, advice and resources for entrepreneurs and managers. It is Ireland's leading business book publisher, with an unrivalled reputation for quality titles across business, management, HR, law, marketing and enterprise topics. NuBooks is its recently-launched imprint, publishing short, focused ebooks for busy entrepreneurs and managers.

In addition, through its founder and managing director, Brian O'Kane, Oak Tree Press occupies a unique position in start-up and small business support in Ireland through its standard-setting titles, as well as training courses, mentoring and advisory services.

Oak Tree Press is comfortable across a range of communication media – print, web and training, focusing always on the effective communication of business information.

Oak Tree Press, 19 Rutland Street, Cork, Ireland.
T: + 353 21 4313855 F: + 353 21 4313496.
E: info@oaktreepress.com W: www.oaktreepress.com.